# THE WAY OF THE SALES SAMURAI: UNLOCKING NEGOTIATION MASTERY

## CJ Benham

**ISBN:** 9798851139918

Orders: Please contact Mildot Media– via enquiries@mildotmedia.com

First Published 2023 by MilDot Media & Sales Samurai

# CONTENTS

# INTRODUCTION

Welcome to your business guide Unlocking Negotiation Mastery.

This guide is unlike any other available on the market and is the first in a series of Sales Samurai performance development guides. Like all our guides, it has been designed to utilise specific training principles which focus on RESULTS.

To use this guide most effectively, try not to dip in and out of chapters, work through the guide start to finish and make use of the any additional study materials available in the market.

I am sure you are more than aware of how competitive it is to become a successful sales professional or deliver a successful sales strategy. Lots of people have taken the opportunity to re-evaluate what is important to them since Covid-19, where they want to pursue their future and in no doubt, starting their own company and working with sales professionals may just be a biproduct of that. Possibly, that may even describe why you have purchased this book?

Sales is not a dirty word. It's a business's lifeblood can be incredibly satisfying and rewarding as a career.

**However, please don't be drawn into the world of social media, celebrities chasing the top 2% of mansion owners and closing phenomenal amounts.**

**This takes years to achieve and too many people start their sales career without the proper set up to reach this level.**

The guide has been written in a chronological format, following the strategies of successful sales professionals. Others are known to take slight variations from this approach and have some success, however, the principles and considerations enclosed will set you in good stead to have a solid foundation on which to build your sales approach. Of course, the caveat is another major pandemic, plague, fire, brimstone or any kind of crazy Armageddon we face after 2023.

Starting a successful sales career is not easy. Only 5 – 10% of initial candidates are hugely successful on reaching their objectives. With many thousands of people striving to achieve this dream, being your own boss with a profitable pipeline takes lots of work, planning and nerves of steel. Central to this guide is the ethos of our training techniques, these are designed to give you the edge over other entrepreneurs and our aim is to help you be successful.

Whilst it would be inappropriate for us to claim an exact blueprint for success, we will provide you with the best practice criteria a professional and profitable sales career.

Thank you for purchasing this guide. I trust you will find it useful and informative. Please do leave feedback on your purchase, your views and opinions are important to me. If you want even greater insight, join our courses online and set yourself apart from the competition.
Best wishes for your future.

CJ Benham
Sales Samurai

# PREFACE BY THE AUTHOR

*Welcome to the definitive guide that will help you become a Successful Negotiator*

Having started both a variety of small businesses, I understand the pressures that will be placed on you and these businesses. In fact, being completely honest with you, it took me three attempts to become a really successful, why? Bad luck, misfortune? Neither the truth was that despite my abilities and what I believed I needed to do, particularly in terms of pricing, what I thought I needed to do and what was actually required by my customers, were set out of sync with each other.

Being a Sales Professional is an immensely challenging, rewarding, difficult and hugely enjoyable job. No two companies are the same, no two weeks are the same and it is this variety and the fast pace of the role that appeals to many people. This is a truly unique industry and starting out that takes more personal commitment and dedication than most people would realise.

After spending several years as both a Special Constable and Business owner, I decided that perhaps this role was not right for me, there was something more I was craving and upon reflection, I didn't really enjoy lots of paperwork (there is a huge amount in that role!). I left the force in the early 2000s and sought to expand my professional skill set in other areas.

My career has developed and grown on the foundations the Police Service instilled in me. But nothing is through chance. To me preparation has become a clear defining factor in terms of success and continual improvement. After leaving the Police Service I have held positions in both small and now global companies. The vast proportion of what I did was regarding Sales, Training and Business Performance Development. This has opened many doors for me and taken me on exciting journeys into various industries and different countries. I have coached both start-ups and multi million-pound established businesses in performance improvement and culture development.

Back in early 2009, I was approached by an expanding provider of careers information guides and e-books. They were looking for a tutor with a proven ability to provide the best courses for their customers. Since May 2009, I delivered ALL of their training courses which were focused on the recruitment processes for various roles. This includes amongst others, Business owner, Firefighter, Paramedic, Train Driver, Magistrate, Army/Navy/RAF Officers. The number of people we personally trained on these courses reached well in excess of 2500 with significant success levels.

Further to this role I went on to write several books regarding personal development in the role of becoming a business owner. It's been a while since my last book was completed.

In 2015 my wife and I, launched our first Detailing Business, growing from start up to £25K turnover in 2 years before restructuring the business in 2019, moving from mobile Detailing Business to fixed location office. Late in 2019 this business successfully secured exclusive rights for the distribution of a UK made cleaning chemicals brand.

Our business was born in December of 2019. Despite Covid19 this has grown month on month with very successful detailing businesses joining our network, using our fantastic product range and benefitting from our face-to-face training and online training courses in building stronger, profitable and viable businesses.  In 2023 we exited from our several of our businesses to concentrate on exciting new ventures.

I have a firm belief that nothing should be left to chance and that true training focuses on the resulting behaviours from the delegate.
What does this mean?

*Just providing information* will enable some delegates to gain success, but it won't empower all to go away from a training course with strategies or reproducible techniques, that are proven to meet the requirements of a successful sales professional.

There are thousands of free resources regarding how to sell etc, and everyone does it slightly differently.

This book isn't aimed at teaching you how to sell, its aimed at how to be exceptional in the specific area of the sales process.

Please work through this guide from the very beginning to the end, despite what you may already know about sales.

We hope you enjoy this book and if you wish to engage with Sales Samurai, you can find us online and on all social media platforms.

Sales Samurai offers business training and consulting services in the area of sales strategy, process and development.

# CHAPTER 1 - THE PHILOSOPHY OF THE SALES SAMURAI

In the world of negotiations, where outcomes are determined by strategies, tactics, and the interactions between parties, the Sales Samurai stands apart. Their approach is rooted in a profound philosophy that encompasses honour, integrity, respect, and a commitment to win-win outcomes. In this chapter, we delve into the core principles that shape the philosophy of the Sales Samurai, providing insights into their mindset and guiding principles that set them apart as master negotiators.

Honour and Integrity:

At the heart of the Sales Samurai's philosophy lies the concept of honour and integrity. The Sales Samurai upholds a code of conduct centred on honesty, transparency, and ethical behaviour. They understand that trust is the cornerstone of successful negotiations and recognise the importance of building and maintaining it. By demonstrating integrity in their actions and words, the Sales Samurai establishes credibility, which paves the way for open and constructive dialogue.

Mastery and Continuous Learning:

The Sales Samurai embraces the path of mastery, recognising that negotiation skills are not innate but honed through practice, study, and experience. They are lifelong learners, constantly seeking to refine their skills and expand their knowledge. By committing to continuous learning, the Sales Samurai remains adaptable and agile, staying abreast of the latest negotiation techniques, market dynamics, and behavioural insights. This dedication to mastery allows them to navigate negotiations with confidence and expertise.

Respect and Empathy:

Central to the Sales Samurai's philosophy is the belief in respect and empathy. They approach negotiations with an open mind, seeking to understand the perspectives, needs, and motivations of all parties involved. The Sales Samurai recognises that every negotiation involves individuals with unique backgrounds, goals, and values. By actively listening and demonstrating empathy, they create an environment of trust and collaboration, fostering a deeper understanding of each party's interests and facilitating creative solutions that meet the needs of all stakeholders.

Win-Win Mindset:

Unlike traditional notions of negotiation as a zero-sum game, the Sales Samurai adopts a win-win mindset. They view negotiations as opportunities to create mutually beneficial outcomes, striving for solutions that address the interests and objectives of all parties involved. The Sales Samurai understands that sustainable success lies in fostering long-term relationships and partnerships rather than short-term gains at the expense of others. By focusing on win-win outcomes, they build trust, encourage collaboration, and lay the foundation for future cooperation.

Adaptability and Flexibility:

In the dynamic landscape of negotiations, the Sales Samurai embraces adaptability and flexibility. They understand that each negotiation is unique, shaped by ever-changing circumstances and variables. The Sales Samurai remains open to alternative approaches, ready to pivot when necessary, and willing to consider diverse perspectives. This adaptability allows them to respond effectively to unexpected challenges, seize opportunities, and find creative solutions that maximize value for all parties involved.

Focus and Preparedness:

Preparation is a fundamental element of the Sales Samurai's philosophy. They believe that success in negotiations is born out of meticulous research, analysis, and strategic planning. By investing time and effort into understanding the industry landscape, gathering relevant information, and assessing the strengths and weaknesses of all parties, the Sales Samurai gains a competitive advantage. Armed with this knowledge, they enter negotiations with clarity, focus, and a well-defined strategy, positioning themselves for success.

Resilience and Perseverance:

Negotiations can be demanding, often filled with obstacles, setbacks, and moments of tension. The Sales Samurai recognises the importance of resilience and perseverance in the face of challenges. They maintain composure, even in the most challenging situations, and exhibit unwavering determination to achieve their goals. By embracing setbacks as learning opportunities and maintaining a positive mindset, the Sales Samurai turns adversity into an advantage, ultimately reaching favourable outcomes.
The philosophy of the Sales Samurai represents.
a powerful and holistic approach to negotiations. It is a philosophy that integrates honour, integrity, respect, empathy, adaptability, and preparedness. By embodying these principles, the Sales Samurai not only achieves exceptional results but also establishes long-lasting relationships built on trust and collaboration.

The philosophy of honour and integrity ensures that the Sales Samurai operates with unwavering honesty and transparency. They understand that trust is the foundation upon which negotiations thrive, and they uphold their reputation as honourable negotiators. This commitment to integrity extends beyond the negotiation table, shaping their interactions and decision-making in all aspects of their professional lives.

Mastery and continuous learning are central tenets of the Sales Samurai's philosophy. They recognise that negotiation skills are developed through deliberate practice and a commitment to ongoing education. By staying abreast of the latest industry trends, behavioural research, and negotiation techniques, they remain at the forefront of their field. This dedication to mastery allows them to navigate even the most complex negotiations with confidence and finesse.

Respect and empathy are integral to the Sales Samurai's approach. They approach negotiations with a genuine desire to understand the perspectives and needs of all parties involved. By actively listening, showing empathy, and considering different viewpoints, they create an atmosphere of mutual respect and collaboration. This empathetic approach fosters open communication, enhances problem-solving, and facilitates the discovery of creative solutions that benefit all stakeholders.

The Sales Samurai's win-win mindset sets them apart from traditional negotiation approaches. Rather than viewing negotiations as a zero-sum game, they seek outcomes that satisfy the interests of all parties involved. This focus on win-win solutions not only creates positive results in the short term but also builds the foundation for sustainable, long-term relationships based on trust and cooperation.

Adaptability and flexibility are critical traits of the Sales Samurai. They understand that negotiations are dynamic and subject to changing circumstances. By remaining open-minded and adaptable, they can adjust their strategies and tactics to align with new information or unexpected developments. This flexibility allows them to seize opportunities and find innovative solutions that may not have been apparent at the outset.

The Sales Samurai's philosophy emphasises the importance of focus and preparedness. They invest considerable time and effort in researching, analysing, and strategizing before entering negotiations. This thorough preparation equips them with a deep understanding of the issues at hand, enabling them to make informed decisions and respond effectively to challenges. Their focus ensures that they stay on course and can navigate complex negotiations with clarity and purpose.

Resilience and perseverance are essential qualities of the Sales Samurai. Negotiations can be fraught with challenges, setbacks, and moments of tension. However, the Sales Samurai maintains composure and demonstrates resilience in the face of adversity. They view setbacks as opportunities for growth, learn from their experiences, and persist in their pursuit of favourable outcomes. Their unwavering determination allows them to overcome obstacles and achieve success even in the most challenging circumstances.

The philosophy of the Sales Samurai embodies a comprehensive and principled approach to negotiations. It combines honour, integrity, respect, empathy, adaptability, and preparedness to create a mindset and skill set that sets them apart as master negotiators. By embracing this philosophy, negotiators can unlock their full potential, foster meaningful relationships, and achieve optimal outcomes in their negotiations. The Sales Samurai's philosophy serves as a guide to navigate the complex world of negotiations with honour, skill, and integrity.

# CHAPTER 2 – THE 5 VIRTUES OF SUCCESSFUL NEGOTIATORS

In the realm of negotiation, success goes beyond mere tactics and strategies. It is the embodiment of virtues that guide negotiators towards achieving optimal outcomes while upholding ethical principles and fostering positive relationships. In this chapter, we explore the five key virtues of successful negotiators, inspired by the spirit of the Sales Samurai. These virtues form the bedrock of their approach, enabling them to navigate negotiations with grace, wisdom, and honour.

Wisdom:

At the core of the Sales Samurai's philosophy is the virtue of wisdom. Successful negotiators possess deep insight and understanding, cultivated through experience and knowledge. They can discern the underlying dynamics of a negotiation, identify hidden opportunities, and make informed decisions that maximize value for all parties involved.

Wise negotiators are adept at analysing complex situations, recognising patterns, and anticipating potential outcomes. They draw upon their wealth of knowledge, staying up to date with industry trends, market dynamics, and behavioural research. This wisdom allows them to make sound judgments, adapt their strategies, and find innovative solutions that align with their objectives and those of their counterparts.

Courage:

Courage is an essential virtue for successful negotiators. It is the willingness to take risks, confront challenges, and navigate difficult conversations with conviction and composure. The Sales Samurai understands that negotiations can be daunting, often involving high stakes, conflicting interests, and moments of tension.

Courageous negotiators are not afraid to speak their minds, assert their positions, or challenge assumptions. They approach negotiations with confidence, staying true to their values and objectives while remaining open to compromise. Their courage enables them to address conflicts, navigate obstacles, and pursue mutually beneficial outcomes, even in the face of uncertainty or adversity.

Empathy:

Empathy is a virtue that lies at the heart of successful negotiations. The Sales Samurai understands the importance of putting oneself in the shoes of others, genuinely seeking to understand their perspectives, needs, and motivations. Empathetic negotiators create an atmosphere of trust and respect, fostering open communication and constructive dialogue.

By actively listening and demonstrating empathy, negotiators can uncover underlying interests and concerns, paving the way for collaborative problem-solving. They show genuine care and consideration for the well-being of all parties involved, recognising that negotiation is not just about reaching an agreement but also about building sustainable relationships based on mutual understanding and shared value.

Integrity:

Integrity is a cornerstone virtue for successful negotiators. The Sales Samurai upholds a code of ethics, operating with honesty, transparency, and a commitment to fairness. They recognise that trust is fragile and hard-earned, and they strive to build and maintain it in all their interactions.

Integrity-driven negotiators keep their promises, follow through on commitments, and avoid deception or manipulation. They approach negotiations with a genuine desire for mutually beneficial outcomes, rather than seeking to exploit or take advantage of others. By embodying integrity, negotiators foster an environment of trust, credibility, and long-term cooperation.

Patience:

Patience is a virtue that distinguishes successful negotiators. The Sales Samurai understands that negotiations can be intricate processes that require time and perseverance. They approach negotiations with a long-term perspective, recognising that rushing or succumbing to impatience can lead to suboptimal outcomes.

Patient negotiators remain calm and composed, even in the face of challenges or delays. They understand that negotiations often involve multiple rounds of discussions, iterations, and compromises. By maintaining patience, negotiators allow the process to unfold naturally, giving space for creative solutions to emerge and for relationships to strengthen over time.

The five virtues of successful negotiators - wisdom, courage, empathy, integrity, and patience - form the foundation of the Sales Samurai philosophy. These virtues guide negotiators in their pursuit of optimal outcomes while upholding ethical principles and fostering positive relationships.

Wisdom enables negotiators to navigate complex negotiations with clarity and insight. It is the product of experience, knowledge, and a deep understanding of the factors at play. Wise negotiators analyse information, anticipate potential outcomes, and make informed decisions that align with their objectives. By drawing upon their wisdom, negotiators can adapt their strategies and find innovative solutions that maximize value for all parties involved.

Courage empowers negotiators to face challenges and take calculated risks. It is the willingness to assert one's positions, challenge assumptions, and address conflicts head-on. Courageous negotiators speak their minds with conviction, maintaining their integrity while remaining open to compromise. With courage, negotiators can navigate difficult conversations, overcome obstacles, and pursue outcomes that satisfy their interests.

Empathy is a virtue that allows negotiators to connect with others on a deeper level. It involves genuine care and consideration for the perspectives, needs, and motivations of all parties involved. Empathetic negotiators actively listen, seek to understand, and validate the feelings and concerns of others. By demonstrating empathy, negotiators foster trust, build rapport, and create an environment conducive to collaborative problem-solving.

Integrity is the bedrock of successful negotiations. It encompasses honesty, transparency, and a commitment to fairness. Negotiators with integrity operate with ethical conduct, keeping their promises, and avoiding deception or manipulation. They approach negotiations with a genuine desire for mutually beneficial outcomes, treating all parties with respect and fairness. By upholding integrity, negotiators cultivate trust and credibility, laying the groundwork for long-term relationships.

Patience is a virtue that allows negotiators to navigate negotiations with a long-term perspective. It is the ability to remain calm, composed, and persistent in the face of challenges or delays. Patient negotiators understand that negotiations require time and multiple iterations. They avoid rushing or succumbing to impatience, giving space for creative solutions to emerge and for relationships to develop. With patience, negotiators can build trust, explore options, and reach mutually satisfactory agreements.

The Sales Samurai embodies these virtues in their approach to negotiations. They recognise that successful negotiations go beyond short-term wins or individual gains. Instead, they focus on long-term relationships, collaborative problem-solving, and ethical conduct. By embracing the virtues of wisdom, courage, empathy, integrity, and patience, negotiators can elevate their practice and achieve outcomes that benefit all parties involved.

Incorporating these virtues into negotiations requires self-reflection, self-discipline, and a commitment to personal growth. Successful negotiators continuously cultivate these virtues through practice, reflection, and learning. They seek feedback, evaluate their actions, and refine their approach to align with their values and goals.

In conclusion, the five virtues of successful negotiators - wisdom, courage, empathy, integrity, and patience - form the ethical compass of the Sales Samurai's philosophy. These virtues guide negotiators to approach negotiations with insight, conviction, empathy, fairness, and resilience. By embodying these virtues, negotiators can foster trust, build strong relationships, and achieve outcomes that not only satisfy their objectives but also contribute to a more harmonious and collaborative world of negotiation.

# CHAPTER 3 - THE ART OF ACTIVE LISTENING IN NEGOTIATIONS

In the realm of negotiation, effective communication is paramount. And at the heart of effective communication lies the art of active listening. The Sales Samurai understands that successful negotiations require not only speaking persuasively but also listening attentively. In this chapter, we delve into the art of active listening and its profound impact on negotiation outcomes. We explore the key principles and techniques that empower negotiators to become skilled listeners and foster open, constructive dialogue.

The Power of Active Listening:

Active listening is more than simply hearing words; it is a deliberate and conscious effort to fully understand the speaker's message. It involves giving undivided attention, observing non-verbal cues, and empathetically connecting with the speaker's perspective. The Sales Samurai recognises that active listening is the key to unlocking valuable insights, building trust, and discovering mutually beneficial solutions.

By actively listening, negotiators demonstrate respect and create a safe space for open communication. They show genuine interest in the speaker's viewpoint, validating their feelings and concerns. This fosters an environment of trust and collaboration, where all parties feel heard and valued. Active listening allows negotiators to uncover underlying interests, clarify misunderstandings, and identify areas of agreement.

Principles of Active Listening:

Give Undivided Attention: Active listening requires undivided attention and a genuine focus on the speaker. Eliminate distractions, both internal and external, and be fully present in the moment. Maintain eye contact, nod, and use verbal and non-verbal cues to indicate your attentiveness.

Suspend Judgment: Avoid prematurely forming opinions or making assumptions. Approach the conversation with an open mind, free from biases or preconceived notions. Suspend judgment and strive to understand the speaker's perspective without imposing your own biases.

Show Empathy: Empathy is a cornerstone of active listening. Put yourself in the speaker's shoes and strive to understand their feelings and concerns. Respond with empathy, acknowledging their emotions, and validating their experiences. This creates a safe and supportive environment for open dialogue.

Ask Clarifying Questions: Active listening involves seeking clarity and deeper understanding. Ask open-ended questions to encourage the speaker to elaborate on their thoughts and feelings. Clarifying questions help to uncover underlying interests, clarify points of confusion, and dig deeper into the underlying issues.

Reflect and Paraphrase: Reflecting and paraphrasing the speaker's words demonstrate active engagement and understanding. Summarize their points, reflect their emotions, and rephrase their statements to ensure accurate comprehension. This not only shows that you are actively listening but also helps to clarify any misunderstandings.

Practice Patience: Active listening requires patience and the willingness to listen beyond surface-level statements. Allow the speaker to express themselves fully without interrupting or rushing to respond. Embrace silence as a tool for reflection and deeper thought.

Techniques for Active Listening:

Mirroring: Mirroring involves repeating or summarizing the speaker's words to confirm understanding and show that you are actively engaged. This technique reinforces the speaker's message and allows for immediate clarification if necessary.

Reflective Listening: Reflective listening involves paraphrasing and reflecting the speaker's emotions and underlying messages. It helps to validate their experiences and shows that you are attuned to their needs and concerns.

Non-Verbal Communication: Non-verbal cues such as maintaining eye contact, nodding, and using facial expressions and gestures can convey active listening. They demonstrate attentiveness and show the speaker that their words are being heard and understood.

Active Silence: Active silence involves purposefully pausing and allowing space for the speaker to gather their thoughts or reflect on their statements. It also allows you to process the information and respond thoughtfully. Active silence encourages the speaker to continue sharing and promotes a deeper level of dialogue.

The Benefits of Active Listening:

Mastering the art of active listening offers numerous benefits in negotiation settings. By embracing this skill, negotiators can:

Gain Deeper Understanding: Active listening allows negotiators to gain a comprehensive understanding of the speaker's perspective, needs, and underlying interests. This deeper understanding enables them to make more informed decisions and develop creative solutions that address the root causes of conflicts.

Build Trust and Rapport: When negotiators actively listen, they create an environment of trust, respect, and empathy. By genuinely engaging with the speaker's thoughts and feelings, negotiators build rapport and foster stronger relationships. This trust serves as a foundation for collaborative problem-solving and the exploration of win-win outcomes.

Uncover Hidden Information: Active listening helps negotiators uncover valuable information that may not be readily apparent. By actively listening to verbal and non-verbal cues, negotiators can identify underlying concerns, unexpressed needs, and potential areas of agreement. This information can be instrumental in crafting creative solutions that satisfy the interests of all parties involved.

Manage Emotions Effectively: Active listening allows negotiators to navigate and manage emotions effectively. By empathetically connecting with the speaker's emotions, negotiators can diffuse tension, validate concerns, and address emotional barriers to reaching agreements. This emotional intelligence enables negotiators to build bridges and find common ground.

Enhance Communication and Problem-Solving: Active listening promotes clear and effective communication between parties. When negotiators truly understand each other's perspectives and interests, they can engage in constructive problem-solving. Active listening fosters a collaborative mindset, encourages the sharing of ideas, and opens possibilities for creative solutions.

Strengthen Negotiation Outcomes: Ultimately, active listening leads to stronger negotiation outcomes. By incorporating the interests and concerns of all parties involved, negotiators can reach agreements that are more durable, mutually beneficial, and sustainable. Active listening allows negotiators to move beyond positional bargaining and focus on finding value-creating solutions.

Practicing Active Listening:

Becoming an active listener requires practice and self-awareness. Here are some practical tips to enhance your active listening skills:

Cultivate Mindfulness: Be fully present in the negotiation setting, focusing your attention on the speaker. Avoid distractions, such as checking emails or thinking about your response.

Develop Empathy: Put yourself in the speaker's shoes and genuinely seek to understand their perspective and emotions. Practice empathy by acknowledging their feelings and demonstrating that you value their input.

Practice Reflective Listening: Use paraphrasing and reflection to ensure accurate understanding of the speaker's message. Summarize their key points and reflect their emotions and underlying interests.

Avoid Interrupting: Allow the speaker to express themselves fully without interruption. Resist the urge to interject or jump to conclusions. Instead, listen attentively and take notes if necessary.

Seek Clarification: Ask open-ended questions to seek clarity and gain a deeper understanding of the speaker's position. This encourages them to elaborate on their thoughts and feelings, providing you with valuable information.

Be Mindful of Non-Verbal Communication: Pay attention to your own non-verbal cues and the non-verbal cues of the speaker. Maintain eye contact, nod to show understanding, and use appropriate facial expressions and gestures to convey engagement.
Conclusion:

Active listening is a powerful tool in the arsenal of successful negotiators. By actively engaging with the speaker, demonstrating empathy, and seeking to understand their perspective, negotiators can unlock valuable insights, build trust, and discover mutually beneficial solutions. The Sales Samurai understands the profound impact of active listening on negotiation outcomes and embraces this art as a cornerstone of their practice. By incorporating the principles and techniques of active listening, negotiators can cultivate deeper understanding, build trust, uncover hidden information, manage emotions effectively, enhance communication and problem-solving, and ultimately achieve stronger negotiation outcomes.

To become an active listener, it is crucial to cultivate mindfulness and be fully present in the negotiation setting. This means eliminating distractions and giving your undivided attention to the speaker. By focusing on the speaker's words, body language, and tone of voice, you can gather a comprehensive understanding of their message.

Empathy plays a vital role in active listening. It involves putting yourself in the speaker's shoes and genuinely seeking to understand their perspective, emotions, and underlying needs. By acknowledging their feelings and concerns, you create a safe and supportive environment for open communication.

Reflective listening is an essential technique for active listening. It involves paraphrasing and reflecting the speaker's words, emotions, and underlying messages. By summarizing their key points and reflecting them back, you demonstrate that you have understood their message and are actively engaged in the conversation. This technique also helps to clarify any misunderstandings and ensures accurate comprehension.

In addition to verbal communication, non-verbal cues are also important in active listening. Maintaining eye contact, nodding to show understanding, and using appropriate facial expressions and gestures convey attentiveness and engagement. Being mindful of your own non-verbal cues and observing the speaker's non-verbal cues can enhance the overall communication process.

Active listening also involves seeking clarification through open-ended questions. By asking thoughtful questions, you encourage the speaker to elaborate on their thoughts, feelings, and interests. This helps to uncover valuable information that may not be readily apparent and allows for a deeper exploration of the issues at hand.

It is important to note that active listening requires patience and the ability to embrace silence. Active silence allows the speaker to gather their thoughts, reflect on their statements, and continue sharing their perspectives. By allowing space for silence, you create an environment that promotes reflection, deeper thought, and more meaningful dialogue.

Practicing active listening requires self-awareness, continuous learning, and commitment. It is a skill that can be developed and honed over time. By incorporating active listening into your negotiation practice, you can enhance your communication skills, build stronger relationships, and achieve more satisfying and sustainable outcomes.

Active Listening is an art that empowers negotiators to fully understand the perspectives of others, build trust, uncover valuable information, manage emotions effectively, enhance communication, and achieve stronger negotiation outcomes. The Sales Samurai recognises the transformative power of active listening and embraces it as a fundamental practice in their approach to negotiations. By embodying the principles and techniques of active listening, negotiators can create an environment of respect, empathy, and collaboration, leading to mutually beneficial agreements and long-lasting relationships.

# CHAPTER 4 – CREATING VALUE THROUGH COLLABORATIVE PROBLEM SOLVING

The Sales Samurai understands that the path to success lies not in a zero-sum game, but in the creation of value for all parties involved. In Chapter 4, we explore the philosophy and techniques of collaborative problem-solving, a fundamental approach that allows negotiators to uncover creative solutions, build consensus, and achieve mutually beneficial outcomes. By embracing this mindset, negotiators can transform conflicts into opportunities for growth and collaboration.

The Philosophy of Collaborative Problem-Solving:

Collaborative problem-solving is rooted in the belief that negotiations are not battles to be won or lost, but collaborative endeavours aimed at finding solutions that meet the interests of all parties involved. The Sales Samurai recognises that by working together and pooling resources, negotiators can create value that exceeds the sum of individual contributions. This philosophy shifts the focus from positional bargaining to a shared exploration of interests and needs.

Key Principles of Collaborative Problem-Solving:

Identify Shared Interests: Collaborative problem-solving begins with the identification of shared interests among the parties involved. By understanding what each party values and seeks to achieve, negotiators can uncover areas of potential agreement and build upon common ground. This process requires active listening, empathy, and an open-minded approach.

Foster Open and Constructive Communication: Effective communication is essential for collaborative problem-solving. By creating an environment where all parties feel safe to express their views and concerns, negotiators encourage open and constructive dialogue. This involves actively listening to each other, valuing diverse perspectives, and reframing differences as opportunities for learning and innovation.

Explore Multiple Options: Collaborative problem-solving encourages the exploration of multiple options and creative solutions. Rather than settling for binary choices, negotiators engage in brainstorming and idea generation to expand the range of possibilities. This process allows for flexibility, innovation, and the discovery of win-win outcomes that meet the interests of all parties involved.

Seek Integrative Solutions: The Sales Samurai understands that integrative solutions, where all parties' interests are met, hold greater long-term value. By searching for mutually beneficial agreements, negotiators avoid zero-sum thinking and strive for outcomes that enhance relationships and create value. This requires a focus on shared goals and a willingness to make trade-offs for the sake of overall success.

Techniques for Collaborative Problem-Solving:

Collaborative Brainstorming: Engage in collaborative brainstorming sessions where all parties are encouraged to contribute ideas and suggestions. By leveraging the collective intelligence of the group, negotiators can uncover innovative solutions that may not have been apparent initially. This process promotes inclusivity, creativity, and the exploration of diverse perspectives.

Interest-Based Negotiation: Move away from positional bargaining and embrace an interest-based approach. By focusing on the underlying needs and interests of all parties, negotiators can identify common ground and generate options that satisfy those interests. This approach promotes collaboration, as negotiators work together to find solutions that address the core concerns of all parties involved.

Problem-Solving Workshops: Organize problem-solving workshops where stakeholders can come together to discuss challenges, share insights, and jointly develop solutions. These workshops provide a platform for collaborative problem-solving, allowing for in-depth discussions and the exchange of expertise. By involving all relevant parties, negotiators can foster a sense of ownership and commitment to the proposed solutions.

Mediation and Facilitation: Consider engaging a neutral third-party mediator or facilitator to guide the negotiation process. A skilled mediator can help manage conflicts, promote effective communication, and facilitate collaborative problem-solving. Their impartial perspective can provide fresh insights and assist in finding creative solutions that satisfy all parties involved.

Benefits of Collaborative Problem-Solving:

Embracing collaborative problem-solving offers numerous benefits in the negotiation process. The Sales Samurai understands that this approach creates a win-win mindset and fosters long-lasting relationships. Here are some key benefits of collaborative problem-solving:

Value Creation: Collaborative problem-solving allows negotiators to create value that goes beyond traditional win-lose outcomes. By exploring interests, brainstorming options, and seeking integrative solutions, negotiators can generate innovative agreements that meet the needs and goals of all parties involved. This value creation leads to more sustainable and mutually beneficial outcomes.

Stronger Relationships: Collaborative problem-solving nurtures stronger relationships among negotiators. By engaging in open and constructive communication, valuing diverse perspectives, and focusing on shared interests, negotiators build trust and rapport. This foundation of trust enhances cooperation, facilitates future negotiations, and creates a positive and productive working environment.

Enhanced Understanding: By actively listening and seeking to understand each other's interests, negotiators gain a deeper understanding of the underlying issues. This understanding allows for better problem identification and the development of more effective solutions. By addressing the root causes of conflicts, negotiators can resolve issues more comprehensively and prevent future disputes.

Increased Satisfaction: Collaborative problem-solving leads to increased satisfaction among all parties involved. When negotiators work together to find solutions that meet their interests, they feel a sense of ownership and investment in the outcome. This satisfaction translates into a higher likelihood of successful implementation and long-term cooperation.

Creative Solutions: Traditional negotiation often limits solutions to a narrow set of options. Collaborative problem-solving encourages out-of-the-box thinking and the exploration of multiple alternatives. By incorporating diverse perspectives and leveraging collective creativity, negotiators can uncover innovative solutions that were previously unseen. This creativity leads to breakthrough agreements that surpass initial expectations.

Improved Decision-Making: Collaborative problem-solving promotes informed and well-considered decision-making. By involving all relevant stakeholders, negotiators can tap into their expertise, experience, and insights. This collaborative decision-making process reduces biases, enhances the quality of decisions, and ensures that all perspectives are considered.

Conflict Resolution: Collaborative problem-solving provides a constructive framework for resolving conflicts. By shifting the focus from adversarial positions to shared interests, negotiators can explore common ground and find mutually acceptable solutions. This approach reduces hostility, defensiveness, and the likelihood of protracted disputes.

Implementing Collaborative Problem-Solving:

To effectively implement collaborative problem-solving, negotiators can consider the following strategies:

Develop a Collaborative Mindset: Cultivate a mindset that values cooperation, mutual respect, and shared interests. Embrace the belief that collaborative problem-solving leads to better outcomes for all parties involved.

Foster a Collaborative Environment: Create an environment that encourages open and constructive communication. Foster a culture of active listening, empathy, and inclusivity. Encourage all parties to contribute their ideas and perspectives.

Seek Common Interests: Identify shared interests among the parties and focus on finding solutions that address those interests. Explore underlying needs and goals to uncover areas of agreement and build consensus.

Promote Effective Communication: Practice active listening, ask clarifying questions, and use reflective techniques to ensure accurate understanding. Encourage transparent and honest communication that fosters trust and understanding.

Embrace Creativity: Encourage brainstorming and the exploration of multiple options. Embrace diverse perspectives and challenge conventional thinking. Foster an atmosphere where innovative solutions are welcomed and appreciated.

Collaborative Decision-Making: Involve all relevant stakeholders in the decision-making process. Seek input and feedback from different perspectives. Strive for consensus-building and shared ownership of the decisions.

Collaborative problem-solving is a powerful approach that allows negotiators to create value, build stronger relationships, and achieve mutually beneficial outcomes. The Sales Samurai recognises the transformative potential of collaborative problem-solving and embraces it as a cornerstone of their negotiation practice. By identifying shared interests, fostering open communication, exploring multiple options, seeking integrative solutions, and promoting a collaborative environment, negotiators can unlock the benefits of this approach.

Collaborative problem-solving goes beyond traditional win-lose dynamics and promotes a win-win mindset where all parties can achieve their objectives. Through active listening, empathy, and a focus on shared interests, negotiators can build trust, enhance understanding, and uncover creative solutions that address the core concerns of all parties involved. This approach not only leads to more satisfying negotiation outcomes but also lays the groundwork for stronger relationships and future collaborations.

To implement collaborative problem-solving effectively, negotiators must cultivate a collaborative mindset and create an environment that supports open and constructive communication. By valuing diverse perspectives, encouraging creativity, and involving all relevant stakeholders, negotiators can tap into the collective intelligence and expertise of the group. This collaborative decision-making process leads to more informed, well-considered decisions that reflect the interests and needs of all parties.

Collaborative problem-solving also offers a valuable framework for conflict resolution. By shifting the focus from adversarial positions to shared interests, negotiators can defuse tension, build common ground, and find mutually acceptable solutions. This approach promotes understanding, reduces hostility, and increases the likelihood of reaching durable agreements.

Collaborative problem-solving is a philosophy and approach that empowers negotiators to create value, foster stronger relationships, and achieve mutually beneficial outcomes. By embracing this mindset, negotiators can move beyond traditional win-lose dynamics and explore innovative solutions that meet the needs and interests of all parties involved. The Sales Samurai recognises the transformative power of collaborative problem-solving and integrates it into their negotiation practice to cultivate sustainable success and build lasting partnerships

# CHAPTER 5 – THE SWORD OF INFLUENCE, BUILDING TRUST & RAPPORT

In the world of negotiation, trust and rapport are invaluable assets that can make or break a deal. The Sales Samurai understands that building strong relationships based on trust is essential for successful negotiations. In Chapter 5, we delve into the philosophy and techniques of building trust and rapport, equipping negotiators with the skills necessary to cultivate meaningful connections and foster mutually beneficial outcomes.

The Importance of Trust in Negotiation:

Trust forms the foundation of effective negotiation. When negotiators trust one another, they are more willing to share information, collaborate, and work towards mutually beneficial solutions. Trust reduces suspicion, increases transparency, and allows negotiators to engage in open and honest communication. Without trust, negotiations can become contentious, unproductive, and hindered by hidden agendas.

The Philosophy of Trust and Rapport:

The Sales Samurai understands that trust is not given freely but earned through consistent actions, integrity, and authenticity. Trust is built on the belief that both parties are committed to creating value and acting in good faith. The Sales Samurai seeks to establish trust as a fundamental principle in all their interactions, recognising that it paves the way for successful negotiations and long-lasting relationships.

Building Trust and Rapport:

Integrity and Ethical Conduct: Demonstrating integrity is paramount in building trust. Honesty, transparency, and ethical conduct are essential. The Sales Samurai follows a strict code of ethics and conducts themselves with utmost integrity, ensuring that their actions align with their words. By upholding ethical standards, negotiators can establish trust and credibility. Active Listening and Empathy: Active listening and empathy are powerful tools in building trust and rapport. By attentively listening to the concerns, needs, and perspectives of others, negotiators show that they value and respect their counterparts. Empathy allows negotiators to understand and appreciate the emotions and experiences of others, creating a connection based on shared understanding.

Consistency and Reliability: Consistency and reliability are crucial in building trust. The Sales Samurai delivers on promises, meets deadlines, and follows through on commitments. By being consistent in their actions and words, negotiators demonstrate their trustworthiness and reliability. Consistency breeds confidence and fosters stronger relationships.

Transparency and Open Communication: Transparency is vital in building trust. Openly sharing relevant information, addressing concerns, and communicating openly and honestly are key components of transparency. The Sales Samurai believes in sharing information openly and avoiding hidden agendas. Transparent communication builds trust and creates a conducive environment for collaboration.

Delivering Value: Trust is also established through delivering value to the other party. The Sales Samurai seeks to understand the interests and needs of their counterparts and actively works towards finding solutions that meet those needs. By consistently delivering value and striving for win-win outcomes, negotiators gain the trust and respect of their counterparts.

Building Personal Connections: Building rapport on a personal level is an essential aspect of trust-building. The Sales Samurai recognises the importance of establishing genuine connections with their counterparts. Finding common ground, sharing experiences, and demonstrating genuine care and interest in others' well-being helps create a bond beyond the negotiation table.

Honouring Confidentiality: Respecting confidentiality and maintaining discretion is crucial in building trust. The Sales Samurai understands the importance of protecting sensitive information and maintains strict confidentiality. By safeguarding confidential information, negotiators instil confidence in their counterparts and build trust.

Resolving Conflicts Constructively: Conflicts are inevitable in negotiations, but how they are handled can either erode or strengthen trust. The Sales Samurai approaches conflicts with a constructive mindset, seeking to understand the underlying issues, and working towards mutually acceptable resolutions. By addressing conflicts openly and collaboratively, negotiators demonstrate their commitment to maintaining trust and preserving the relationship.

Benefits of Building Trust and Rapport:

Building trust and rapport in negotiations offers a range of benefits that contribute to successful outcomes. The Sales Samurai understands these benefits and actively cultivates trust to unlock their potential:

Enhanced Collaboration: Trust fosters an environment of collaboration where negotiators feel comfortable sharing information, ideas, and concerns. This collaborative atmosphere promotes joint problem-solving, creativity, and the exploration of win-win solutions. Negotiators can leverage their collective expertise and perspectives, leading to more comprehensive and innovative outcomes.

Improved Communication: Trust enables open and effective communication. When negotiators trust one another, they are more likely to express their thoughts, feelings, and needs honestly and directly. This open communication reduces misunderstandings, avoids misinterpretations, and facilitates a clearer understanding of each party's interests and objectives.

Efficient Decision-Making: Building trust streamlines the decision-making process. When negotiators trust one another, they can rely on the information and proposals put forward. This trust accelerates the decision-making process as parties can confidently make choices based on the credibility and reliability of their counterparts. Efficient decision-making ensures progress and prevents unnecessary delays.

Greater Flexibility and Adaptability: Trust allows negotiators to be more flexible and adaptable in their approach. When parties trust one another's intentions, they are more willing to explore alternative options and consider compromises. This flexibility allows negotiators to adapt to changing circumstances, accommodate unforeseen challenges, and find mutually beneficial solutions even in complex situations.

Strengthened Relationships: Building trust and rapport nurtures stronger and more meaningful relationships. By investing time and effort in building trust, negotiators develop a foundation of mutual respect, understanding, and appreciation. These strong relationships extend beyond the negotiation at hand and lay the groundwork for future collaborations and partnerships. Increased Confidence: Trust instils confidence in negotiators. When parties trust one another, they can approach negotiations with a sense of assurance and security. This confidence empowers negotiators to make bolder proposals, engage in constructive discussions, and take calculated risks, knowing that the other party is acting in good faith.

Conflict Resolution: Trust plays a pivotal role in resolving conflicts effectively. When conflicts arise, a foundation of trust enables negotiators to engage in open and honest dialogue, facilitating a deeper exploration of the underlying issues. Trust reduces defensiveness and fosters a collaborative mindset, allowing parties to find mutually acceptable solutions and preserve the relationship despite differences.

Strategies for Building Trust and Rapport:

Invest in Relationship Building: Allocate time and effort to building relationships beyond the negotiation table. Seek opportunities for social interactions, such as informal gatherings or shared activities, to establish personal connections and foster rapport.

Demonstrate Authenticity: Be genuine and authentic in your interactions. Show a sincere interest in the well-being and perspectives of others. Avoid manipulative tactics or deceptive practices that can erode trust. Transparency and authenticity are key to building and maintaining trust.

Be Reliable and Consistent: Consistently deliver on your commitments and promises. Build a reputation for reliability and follow-through. Demonstrating consistency in your words and actions builds trust and instils confidence in your counterparts.

Communicate Clearly and Honestly: Maintain open lines of communication and be transparent in sharing information. Communicate clearly, avoiding ambiguity or mixed messages. Honesty and transparency breed trust and facilitate effective negotiation.

Practice Active Listening: Actively listen to the concerns, needs, and perspectives of others. Show genuine interest and understanding by asking clarifying questions and paraphrasing to ensure accurate comprehension. Active listening demonstrates respect and empathy, strengthening the foundation of trust.

Honour Confidentiality: Respect the confidentiality of sensitive information shared during negotiations. Establish clear boundaries and protocols for handling confidential information. Respecting confidentiality builds trust and reassures parties that their information will be handled with utmost discretion.

Seek Win-Win Solutions: Demonstrate a genuine commitment to finding mutually beneficial solutions. Show that you are not solely focused on your own interests but also considerate of the needs and goals of the other party. By actively seeking win-win outcomes, you build trust and foster a collaborative mindset.

Address Concerns and Conflict Promptly: When conflicts or concerns arise, address them promptly and constructively. Avoid ignoring or dismissing issues, as this can erode trust. Instead, engage in open dialogue, actively listen to each party's perspective, and work towards finding mutually acceptable resolutions.

Display Empathy and Understanding: Cultivate empathy and understanding towards the experiences and emotions of others. Put yourself in their shoes and strive to understand their perspectives and underlying motivations. Demonstrating empathy builds rapport and strengthens trust by showing that you genuinely care about the well-being and interests of the other party.

Be Open to Feedback and Collaboration: Foster an environment where feedback is encouraged, and collaboration is valued. Welcome input from others and demonstrate a willingness to incorporate their ideas and suggestions. By being open to feedback and collaboration, you foster a sense of ownership and shared responsibility, which contributes to building trust.

Building trust and rapport is a fundamental aspect of successful negotiations. The Sales Samurai recognises that trust forms the bedrock of effective communication, collaboration, and relationship building. By embracing the philosophy of trust and employing strategies such as integrity, active listening, transparency, and empathy, negotiators can cultivate meaningful connections and foster mutually beneficial outcomes. Trust enhances collaboration, decision-making, and conflict resolution, leading to stronger relationships and increased satisfaction for all parties involved. The Sales Samurai integrates the principles of trust and rapport into their negotiation practice, paving the way for successful outcomes and long-term partnerships.

# CHAPTER 6 – EMOTIONAL INTELLIGENCE IN NEGOTIATION

Emotions play a significant role in negotiations, shaping the dynamics, decision-making, and outcomes. The Sales Samurai understands the importance of emotional intelligence in navigating the complex landscape of negotiations. In Chapter 6, we delve into the philosophy and techniques of emotional intelligence, equipping negotiators with the skills necessary to recognise, understand, and manage emotions effectively to achieve favourable results.

The Significance of Emotional Intelligence:

Emotional intelligence refers to the ability to recognise, understand, and manage one's own emotions and the emotions of others. In negotiation, emotions can impact the decision-making process, communication, and relationship dynamics. Emotional intelligence empowers negotiators to navigate these emotional landscapes with poise, empathy, and self-awareness, leading to more successful outcomes and enhanced relationships.

The Philosophy of Emotional Intelligence:

The Sales Samurai believes that emotional intelligence is a crucial element of effective negotiation. By embracing emotional intelligence, negotiators can better understand the underlying motivations, concerns, and desires of all parties involved. This understanding allows negotiators to adapt their communication styles, manage emotions effectively, and foster an environment that promotes collaboration and win-win solutions.

Key Elements of Emotional Intelligence:

Self-Awareness: Self-awareness is the foundation of emotional intelligence. The Sales Samurai emphasises the importance of self-reflection and introspection to recognise one's own emotions, triggers, and biases. By understanding their own emotional states, negotiators can better manage their reactions and make informed decisions.

Empathy: Empathy is the ability to understand and share the emotions of others. The Sales Samurai encourages negotiators to put themselves in the shoes of their counterparts, seeking to understand their perspectives, needs, and concerns. By demonstrating empathy, negotiators can build rapport, establish trust, and foster a collaborative environment.

Emotional Regulation: Emotional regulation involves managing and controlling one's emotions effectively. The Sales Samurai recognises that negotiators must navigate through various emotions, such as frustration, disappointment, or excitement, without allowing them to cloud judgment or derail the negotiation process. By cultivating emotional regulation, negotiators can make rational decisions and maintain a constructive negotiation atmosphere.

Social Awareness: Social awareness involves recognising and understanding the emotions and dynamics of others. The Sales Samurai encourages negotiators to pay attention to non-verbal cues, listen actively, and interpret the emotions expressed by their counterparts. Social awareness allows negotiators to adjust their approach, tailor their communication, and address the emotional needs of the other party.

Relationship Management: Relationship management focuses on building and maintaining productive relationships. The Sales Samurai emphasises the importance of establishing open lines of communication, fostering trust, and resolving conflicts effectively. By managing relationships with emotional intelligence, negotiators can create an environment conducive to collaboration and mutual success.

Techniques for Applying Emotional Intelligence in Negotiation:

Self-Reflection and Awareness: Engage in self-reflection to identify your own emotional triggers, biases, and assumptions. Regularly assess your emotional state and its impact on your negotiation approach. By understanding your own emotions, you can manage them effectively and make informed decisions.

Active Listening and Empathy: Practice active listening to truly understand the perspectives and emotions of others. Put yourself in their shoes and demonstrate empathy. By acknowledging and validating their emotions, you can establish a connection, build rapport, and foster understanding.

Recognise and Label Emotions: Develop the ability to recognise and label your own emotions and those of others. By accurately identifying emotions, you can respond appropriately and adjust your communication style. Labelling emotions helps create a shared understanding and facilitates effective dialogue.

Emotional Regulation Techniques: Implement strategies to regulate your own emotions during negotiations. Techniques such as deep breathing, taking breaks, or reframing negative thoughts can help you maintain composure, make rational decisions, and prevent emotional reactions from derailing the negotiation process. By managing your emotions effectively, you can stay focused on the desired outcomes.

Use Emotional Intelligence to Influence: Leverage emotional intelligence to influence the emotions and perspectives of others. By demonstrating empathy, understanding, and genuine care, you can create a positive emotional climate that encourages cooperation and collaboration. Skilful use of emotional intelligence can help sway opinions, build trust, and foster mutually beneficial solutions.

Adapt Communication Styles: Tailor your communication style to accommodate the emotional needs and preferences of your counterparts. Some individuals may respond better to a direct and assertive approach, while others may require a more empathetic and collaborative approach. Adapting your communication style fosters effective engagement and understanding.

Respond, Don't React: Practice responding to emotions rather than reacting impulsively. Take a moment to assess the situation, consider the impact of your response, and choose a thoughtful and constructive course of action. Responding with emotional intelligence allows you to navigate challenging moments with grace and professionalism.

Collaborative Problem-Solving: Apply emotional intelligence to encourage collaborative problem-solving. By creating an environment where all parties feel heard, understood, and valued, you can foster a sense of ownership and shared responsibility for finding solutions. Emotional intelligence helps manage conflicts, find common ground, and explore win-win outcomes. Build and Maintain Relationships: Emotional intelligence plays a vital role in building and maintaining strong relationships. Show genuine interest in the well-being and success of your counterparts. Nurture trust, respect, and open communication. Invest time and effort in building long-term relationships based on mutual understanding and collaboration. Benefits of Applying Emotional Intelligence in Negotiation:

Improved Communication: Emotional intelligence enhances communication by facilitating understanding and empathy. It helps negotiators interpret non-verbal cues, listen actively, and adapt their communication style to resonate with their counterparts. This leads to clearer and more effective communication, reducing misunderstandings and fostering productive dialogue.

Enhanced Relationship Building: Emotional intelligence strengthens relationships by establishing trust, rapport, and mutual respect. When negotiators understand and respond to the emotional needs of others, it creates a supportive environment for collaboration and problem-solving. Strong relationships pave the way for long-term partnerships and successful future negotiations.

Conflict Resolution: Emotional intelligence enables negotiators to navigate conflicts with sensitivity and understanding. By managing emotions and demonstrating empathy, negotiators can de-escalate conflicts, find common ground, and work towards mutually acceptable resolutions. This promotes positive outcomes and preserves the relationship.

Decision-Making: Emotional intelligence enhances decision-making by balancing rationality with emotional awareness. By understanding the impact of emotions on judgment, negotiators can make more informed and objective decisions. Emotional intelligence allows negotiators to consider the emotional implications of their choices and make decisions that align with their objectives and values.

Increased Satisfaction: Applying emotional intelligence in negotiation leads to increased satisfaction for all parties involved. When negotiators demonstrate empathy, understanding, and a willingness to find mutually beneficial solutions, it fosters a sense of fairness and cooperation. This leads to outcomes that meet the needs and interests of all parties, enhancing overall satisfaction.

Emotional intelligence is a powerful tool for negotiators, enabling them to navigate the intricate landscape of emotions with finesse and empathy. The Sales Samurai recognises that emotional intelligence is essential for understanding and managing emotions effectively, building relationships, and achieving successful negotiation outcomes. By embracing self-awareness, empathy, emotional regulation, social awareness, and relationship management, negotiators can leverage emotional intelligence to communicate effectively, resolve conflicts, and make informed decisions. Integrating emotional intelligence into negotiation practices not only enhances individual effectiveness but also fosters a collaborative and harmonious negotiation environment. The Sales Samurai embodies the philosophy of emotional intelligence, equipping negotiators with the skills to recognise and manage emotions effectively, fostering successful outcomes and strengthening relationships.

In the following chapters, we will explore the concept of strategic thinking in negotiation. Strategic thinking is a crucial mindset that empowers negotiators to analyse complex situations, anticipate potential challenges, and develop well-informed plans to achieve their objectives. The Sales Samurai understands the importance of strategic thinking and its impact on negotiation success. Stay tuned as we delve into the philosophy and strategies of strategic thinking in the art of negotiation.

# CHAPTER 7 – NAVIGATING CONFLICT: SAMUARI CONFLICT RESOLUTION TECHNIQUES

Conflict is an inevitable part of negotiations, and the Sales Samurai understands that navigating conflicts effectively is crucial for successful outcomes. In Chapter 7, we explore the philosophy and techniques of conflict resolution inspired by the wisdom of the Samurai. By embracing these conflict resolution techniques, negotiators can manage conflicts with grace, preserve relationships, and create win-win solutions.

The Philosophy of Conflict Resolution:

The Sales Samurai recognises that conflicts are opportunities for growth and transformation. Instead of viewing conflicts as obstacles, negotiators can adopt a mindset that embraces conflicts as a catalyst for deeper understanding, creativity, and collaboration. The philosophy of conflict resolution emphasises the importance of seeking mutual understanding, fostering open communication, and finding common ground to reach resolutions that satisfy the interests of all parties involved.

Samurai Conflict Resolution Techniques:

Mindful Awareness:
The Sales Samurai believes in cultivating mindful awareness during conflicts. Mindfulness involves being fully present in the moment, observing one's own thoughts and emotions without judgment. By developing mindful awareness, negotiators can detach themselves from reactive responses and approach conflicts with clarity and calmness. Mindfulness allows negotiators to respond thoughtfully, consider alternative perspectives, and find common ground for resolution.

Active Listening:
Active listening is a powerful tool in conflict resolution. The Sales Samurai emphasises the importance of truly hearing and understanding the concerns, needs, and perspectives of all parties involved. Through active listening, negotiators can demonstrate empathy, validate emotions, and build rapport. Active listening creates a safe space for open communication, enabling negotiators to uncover underlying interests and generate creative solutions.

Effective Communication:
Effective communication is essential for resolving conflicts. The Sales Samurai encourages negotiators to communicate clearly, assertively, and respectfully. Expressing needs, concerns, and interests in a constructive manner fosters understanding and facilitates collaborative problem-solving. Effective communication also involves using non-verbal cues, such as body language and tone of voice, to convey sincerity and openness.

Win-Win Solutions:
The Sales Samurai believes in the power of win-win solutions, where all parties involved can achieve their objectives and interests. Rather than seeking to dominate or defeat the other party, negotiators should strive for mutually beneficial outcomes. By focusing on shared interests, exploring creative options, and engaging in collaborative problem-solving, negotiators can generate win-win solutions that satisfy everyone involved.

Mediation and Facilitation:

The Sales Samurai recognises the value of mediation and facilitation techniques in resolving conflicts. Mediation involves the assistance of a neutral third party to guide the negotiation process, promote understanding, and facilitate communication between the conflicting parties. A skilled mediator helps create an environment of trust and assists in finding common ground for resolution. Negotiators can employ facilitation techniques themselves or seek the help of a trained mediator to navigate conflicts effectively.

Emotional Intelligence:
Emotional intelligence plays a vital role in conflict resolution. The Sales Samurai emphasises the importance of recognising and managing emotions during conflicts. By practicing self-awareness and empathy, negotiators can understand their own emotional triggers and those of others. Emotional intelligence enables negotiators to respond to conflicts with composure, address emotional needs, and defuse tense situations, leading to constructive dialogue and resolution.

Compromise and Collaboration:
The Sales Samurai acknowledges that compromise and collaboration are essential elements of conflict resolution. While maintaining individual interests, negotiators must be willing to make concessions and find middle ground. Collaboration involves seeking input from all parties, integrating diverse perspectives, and working towards a solution that benefits everyone. The Sales Samurai encourages negotiators to prioritise long-term relationships over short-term gains.

Respect and Cultural Sensitivity:
Respect and cultural sensitivity are fundamental in conflict resolution. The Sales Samurai recognises the importance of valuing diverse viewpoints and treating all parties with respect. Cultural differences can impact conflict resolution styles and approaches. Negotiators must be mindful of cultural norms, customs, and communication styles, adapting their approach to ensure inclusivity and understanding. Respecting cultural differences promotes a harmonious negotiation environment and paves the way for effective conflict resolution.

Focus on the Problem, Not the Person:
The Sales Samurai advises negotiators to separate the problem from the person during conflicts. By shifting the focus from personal attacks to a collaborative problem-solving mindset, negotiators can foster a more productive atmosphere. Addressing the problem rather than attacking individuals allows for a constructive discussion of the issues at hand, enabling parties to work towards mutually beneficial solutions.

Forgiveness and Moving Forward:
Forgiveness and the ability to move forward are integral aspects of conflict resolution. The Sales Samurai believes in letting go of past grievances and focusing on the future. By practicing forgiveness, negotiators can release negative emotions and create space for healing and reconciliation. Moving forward with a positive mindset allows for renewed collaboration and a fresh start in the negotiation process.

Benefits of Samurai Conflict Resolution Techniques:

Preserving Relationships:
By employing Samurai conflict resolution techniques, negotiators can preserve and strengthen relationships. Open communication, active listening, and mutual respect build trust and understanding, fostering long-term partnerships beyond the current negotiation. Maintaining positive relationships ensures future collaboration and successful outcomes.

Creative Problem-Solving:
Samurai conflict resolution techniques encourage creative problem-solving. By focusing on win-win solutions, negotiators explore alternative options and generate innovative ideas. Collaboration and compromise lead to outcomes that satisfy the interests of all parties involved, creating value, and maximizing mutual benefits.

Enhancing Decision-Making:
Conflict resolution techniques enable negotiators to make informed and objective decisions. By considering diverse perspectives and engaging in constructive dialogue, negotiators gain a broader understanding of the issues at hand. This comprehensive view enhances decision-making,

ensuring that choices align with the desired outcomes and contribute to long-term success.

Strengthening Trust and Rapport:
Effective conflict resolution techniques build trust and rapport between parties. When conflicts are managed with mindfulness, empathy, and respect, it establishes a foundation of trust and mutual understanding. Strengthening trust enhances communication, collaboration, and future negotiation efforts.

Personal Growth and Development:
The practice of Samurai conflict resolution techniques fosters personal growth and development. Negotiators become more self-aware, empathetic, and skilled communicators. By embracing conflict as an opportunity for learning and growth, negotiators enhance their ability to navigate challenging situations, both in negotiations and in other aspects of life.

Conflict resolution is an essential skill for negotiators, and the Sales Samurai provides a philosophy and techniques inspired by the wisdom of the Samurai. By practicing mindful awareness, active listening, effective communication, and seeking win-win solutions, negotiators can navigate conflicts with grace and preserve relationships. Incorporating mediation, emotional intelligence, compromise, and cultural sensitivity promotes collaborative problem-solving and paves the way for successful outcomes.

The Sales Samurai believes that conflict resolution techniques not only lead to effective negotiation but also foster personal growth, enhance decision-making, and build strong and enduring relationships. In the next chapter, we will explore the art of strategic thinking, equipping negotiators with the mindset and strategies necessary to analyse complex situations and achieve their objectives.

# CHAPTER 8 – CRAFTING WIN:WIN SOLUTIONS; SAMURAI COLLABORATION STRATEGIES

In the art of negotiation, the Sales Samurai understands the significance of crafting win-win solutions that satisfy the interests of all parties involved. Chapter 8 explores the philosophy and strategies of collaboration inspired by the wisdom of the Samurai. By embracing these collaboration strategies, negotiators can foster a cooperative environment, promote creativity, and generate outcomes that maximize mutual benefits.

The Philosophy of Collaboration:

The Sales Samurai believes in the power of collaboration to achieve harmonious and sustainable outcomes. Collaboration goes beyond compromise or concession; it is an approach that seeks to integrate diverse perspectives, leverage shared interests, and create solutions that go beyond mere agreement. The philosophy of collaboration emphasises open communication, trust-building, and a focus on mutual gains for all parties involved.

Samurai Collaboration Strategies:

Shared Vision:
The Sales Samurai recognises the importance of a shared vision in collaboration. Negotiators should strive to create a common understanding of the desired outcome, aligning their goals and aspirations. By establishing a shared vision, negotiators can foster a sense of purpose and commitment, driving them towards collaborative problem-solving and win-win solutions.

Open Communication:
Effective collaboration relies on open and transparent communication. The Sales Samurai encourages negotiators to share information freely, express their needs and concerns, and actively listen to others. Transparent communication builds trust and ensures that all parties have a comprehensive understanding of the issues at hand. It also encourages the exploration of creative ideas and promotes collaborative decision-making.

Creative Problem-Solving:
The Sales Samurai believes in the power of creative problem-solving to uncover innovative solutions. Collaborative negotiation involves thinking outside the box, considering multiple perspectives, and exploring alternative options. By embracing creativity, negotiators can transcend traditional solutions and find new ways to address complex challenges. Creative problem-solving opens doors to win-win outcomes that maximize value for all parties involved.

Trust and Rapport:
Trust and rapport are essential elements of successful collaboration. The Sales Samurai emphasises the importance of building trust among negotiators. Trust enables open communication, facilitates information sharing, and encourages cooperation. Building rapport through empathy, active listening, and respect establishes a solid foundation for collaboration and strengthens the negotiation process.

Consensus Building:

Consensus building is a critical strategy for collaboration. The Sales Samurai encourages negotiators to seek agreement through mutual understanding and shared decision-making. Consensus building involves engaging all parties, incorporating their perspectives, and finding common ground that satisfies the interests of everyone involved. By striving for consensus, negotiators create a sense of ownership and commitment, increasing the likelihood of successful implementation.

Flexibility and Adaptability:
Collaboration requires flexibility and adaptability. The Sales Samurai advises negotiators to be open to change and willing to adjust their positions. Flexibility allows negotiators to respond to new information, adapt to evolving circumstances, and explore innovative solutions. By embracing flexibility, negotiators demonstrate their commitment to collaboration and their willingness to find mutually beneficial outcomes.

Win-Win Mindset:
The Sales Samurai advocates for a win-win mindset in collaboration. Rather than focusing on competition or zero-sum outcomes, negotiators should approach collaboration with the belief that there are opportunities for all parties to achieve their objectives. A win-win mindset fosters a positive negotiation environment, encourages creative problem-solving, and promotes long-term relationships.

Empathy and Perspective-Taking:
Empathy and perspective-taking are fundamental aspects of collaboration. The Sales Samurai encourages negotiators to understand the needs, interests, and perspectives of others. By putting themselves in the shoes of their counterparts, negotiators can cultivate empathy, build trust, and find solutions that address the concerns of all parties involved. Empathy and perspective-taking create an inclusive negotiation environment that promotes collaboration and cooperation.

9. Integrating Diverse Perspectives:

Collaboration thrives when diverse perspectives are integrated into the decision-making process. The Sales Samurai recognises the value of inclusivity and encourages negotiators to embrace diversity in thoughts, experiences, and backgrounds. Integrating diverse perspectives brings fresh ideas to the table, challenges assumptions, and fosters a more comprehensive understanding of the negotiation context. By actively seeking diverse viewpoints, negotiators can create solutions that consider a wide range of factors and maximize the potential for successful outcomes.

Conflict Resolution:
Conflicts may arise during collaboration, but the Sales Samurai understands that effective conflict resolution is crucial for maintaining the collaborative spirit. Negotiators should approach conflicts with the intention of finding mutually acceptable solutions. They should engage in constructive dialogue, actively listen to each other's concerns, and seek common ground through compromise and open-mindedness. Resolving conflicts promptly and respectfully ensures that the collaborative process remains intact and progress towards a win-win solution continues.

Benefits of Samurai Collaboration Strategies:

Enhanced Problem-Solving:
By incorporating Samurai collaboration strategies, negotiators can enhance their problem-solving abilities. Creative thinking, open communication, and integration of diverse perspectives lead to comprehensive and innovative solutions. Collaborative problem-solving maximizes the potential for addressing complex challenges effectively, leading to more robust and sustainable outcomes.

Strengthened Relationships:
Collaboration builds strong and lasting relationships among negotiators. Through open communication, trust-building, and shared decision-making, negotiators develop a sense of camaraderie and mutual respect. These positive relationships extend beyond the negotiation table and lay the foundation for future collaborations, fostering long-term partnerships and shared successes.

Increased Value Creation:

Collaboration is a powerful driver of value creation. By leveraging shared interests, exploring creative options, and finding win-win solutions, negotiators can unlock additional value that may not have been apparent in a competitive approach. Collaboration allows for the identification of mutually beneficial opportunities and the generation of outcomes that maximize value for all parties involved.

Improved Implementation:
When all parties are actively involved in the decision-making process, the likelihood of successful implementation increases. Collaborative solutions are more likely to be embraced by all stakeholders, as they reflect a collective effort and consider the needs and perspectives of each party. This leads to smoother implementation, reduced resistance, and a higher chance of achieving desired outcomes.

Personal Growth and Development:
Practicing collaboration strategies inspired by the Sales Samurai fosters personal growth and development. Negotiators cultivate skills such as active listening, empathy, creative thinking, and adaptability, which can be applied not only in negotiations but also in various aspects of life. Collaboration promotes self-awareness, flexibility, and the ability to navigate complex situations with grace and effectiveness.

Collaboration is a cornerstone of successful negotiation, and the Sales Samurai offers a philosophy and strategies to foster collaborative environments. By embracing shared vision, open communication, creative problem-solving, and consensus-building, negotiators can craft win-win solutions that maximize mutual benefits. Trust, flexibility, empathy, and the integration of diverse perspectives further enhance collaboration. The benefits of collaboration extend beyond individual negotiations, strengthening relationships, creating value, and promoting personal growth. In the next chapter, we will explore the art of ethical persuasion, equipping negotiators with the skills to influence and persuade others in a principled and respectful manner.

# Chapter 9: PREPARING FOR BATTLE: RESEARCH AND STRATEGY FOR SALES SAMURAI

In this chapter we delve into the critical aspect of preparation for Sales Samurai negotiations. As a Sales Samurai, one must approach negotiations like a strategic battle, armed with knowledge, insights, and a well-defined strategy. This chapter focuses on the importance of thorough research and effective strategizing to lay the foundation for successful negotiations. By understanding the significance of preparation and adopting the Sales Samurai mindset, negotiators can gain a competitive edge and increase their chances of achieving favourable outcomes.

The Art of Research:
Research forms the bedrock of effective negotiation preparation. Sales Samurai understand that thorough research enables them to gain valuable insights into the parties involved, their interests, industry dynamics, market trends, and potential areas of leverage. They dig deep to gather information from diverse sources, including company reports, industry publications, market analysis, and social media platforms. Armed with this knowledge,

Sales Samurai are well-equipped to craft informed strategies and tailor their negotiation approach to the specific context.

Identifying Stakeholders:
Stakeholder analysis is a crucial component of negotiation preparation. Sales Samurai meticulously identifies and analyse the key stakeholders involved in the negotiation process. They consider the perspectives, interests, and power dynamics among various stakeholders. By understanding the motivations and priorities of each stakeholder, Sales Samurai can devise strategies that appeal to their individual needs and create alignment among the parties involved.

Setting Objectives and Priorities:
Sales Samurai approach negotiations with clear objectives and priorities in mind. They define what they aim to achieve and outline the desired outcomes of the negotiation. Whether it's securing a strategic partnership, achieving a favourable deal structure, or resolving a conflict, Sales Samurai align their strategy with their objectives. They prioritise their goals, identifying the must-haves, nice-to-haves, and areas of flexibility. This clarity enables them to focus their efforts and resources effectively during the negotiation process.

Analysing the BATNA:
The Best Alternative to a Negotiated Agreement (BATNA) is a critical element in negotiation preparation. Sales Samurai meticulously analyse their BATNA, which represents the course of action they will pursue if the negotiation does not result in a favourable outcome. By evaluating their BATNA, Sales Samurai assess the strength of their position and leverage during negotiations. This analysis empowers them to make informed decisions, evaluate potential trade-offs, and navigate the negotiation process strategically.

Crafting a Value Proposition:
Sales Samurai understand the importance of presenting a compelling value proposition to the other party. They meticulously analyse their own strengths, unique selling points, and the value they can offer to the other party. By identifying the specific benefits and advantages they bring to the

table, Sales Samurai effectively communicate their value proposition, differentiating themselves from competitors and building a strong case for collaboration or agreement.

Assessing the Negotiation Context:
Understanding the broader context in which the negotiation takes place is crucial for Sales Samurai. They analyse factors such as market conditions, industry trends, regulatory frameworks, and potential external influences that may impact the negotiation process. This contextual understanding enables Sales Samurai to anticipate challenges, identify potential opportunities, and adapt their strategies accordingly.

Scenario Planning:
Sales Samurai engage in scenario planning to anticipate various outcomes and devise appropriate responses. They consider multiple scenarios, ranging from ideal outcomes to challenging situations, and develop strategies to address each possibility. This proactive approach allows them to be agile and responsive during negotiations, adjusting their tactics based on the unfolding dynamics of the negotiation process.

Building Relationships and Trust:
Sales Samurai recognise the significance of building relationships and fostering trust before entering into negotiations. They invest time in networking, establishing rapport, and understanding the interests and concerns of the other party. By nurturing relationships and building trust, Sales Samurai create an environment of collaboration and open communication during negotiations. They aim to build a foundation of trust that allows for transparent discussions and mutually beneficial outcomes.

Developing Counterarguments:
Sales Samurai anticipate potential objections and counterarguments from the other party and prepare thoughtful responses in advance. They analyse the interests and concerns of the other party and develop persuasive arguments to address them effectively. By preparing well-crafted counterarguments, Sales Samurai demonstrate their thorough understanding of the negotiation dynamics and their ability to address concerns and objections in a compelling manner.

Crafting a Communication Strategy:
Effective communication is a cornerstone of successful negotiations. Sales Samurai develop a communication strategy that aligns with their objectives and the preferences of the other party. They consider factors such as the communication style, cultural nuances, and potential barriers to effective communication. By tailoring their communication approach, Sales Samurai ensure clarity, understanding, and alignment between the parties involved.

Practicing and Rehearsing:
Sales Samurai understand the importance of practice and rehearsal before entering into negotiations. They simulate negotiation scenarios, engage in role plays, and seek feedback from trusted colleagues or mentors. This practice allows them to refine their negotiation skills, test their strategies, and build confidence. By investing time in practice, Sales Samurai are better prepared to navigate the dynamics of the negotiation process with agility and poise.

By conducting thorough research, analysing stakeholders, setting clear objectives, and crafting effective strategies, Sales Samurai lay the groundwork for successful negotiations. They understand the value of comprehensive preparation in gaining insights, identifying leverage points, and building trust with the other party. Through meticulous preparation and a strategic mindset, Sales Samurai position themselves for favourable outcomes and demonstrate their mastery in the art of negotiation. By adopting these practices and investing in thorough preparation, negotiators can enhance their negotiation skills and achieve greater success in their professional endeavours.

# Chapter 10: THE WAY OF SILENCE: HARNESSING THE POWER OF PAUSE

In the realm of negotiation, the Sales Samurai recognises the profound impact of silence and the art of the pause. Chapter 10 delves into the philosophy of harnessing the power of silence to enhance communication, gain insights, and achieve favourable outcomes. The Sales Samurai understands that silence can be a powerful tool, allowing negotiators to listen attentively, gather information, and respond strategically. By mastering the way of silence, negotiators can navigate negotiations with greater clarity, wisdom, and effectiveness.

The Power of Silence:

Silence is often undervalued and overlooked in negotiations, but the Sales Samurai embraces its transformative potential. Silence provides a space for reflection, deep listening, and the cultivation of mindfulness. It allows negotiators to gather their thoughts, observe non-verbal cues, and create openings for meaningful dialogue. The power of silence lies in its ability to foster understanding, defuse tension, and invite thoughtful responses.

Harnessing the Power of Pause:

Active Listening:
Silence plays a vital role in active listening, one of the core skills of effective negotiation. By pausing and attentively listening to the words and emotions of others, negotiators can gain valuable insights and understand the underlying interests and concerns. Active listening involves suspending judgment, avoiding interruptions, and creating a safe space for open and honest communication. The Sales Samurai encourages negotiators to harness the power of silence to engage in active listening, promoting mutual understanding and building trust.

Strategic Reflection:
Silence provides an opportunity for strategic reflection during negotiations. By taking a moment to pause and reflect, negotiators can gather their thoughts, assess the situation, and formulate well-considered responses. Strategic reflection allows for the evaluation of options, the identification of potential pitfalls, and the generation of creative solutions. The Sales Samurai advises negotiators to embrace silence as a means to strategically navigate negotiations and make informed decisions.

Defusing Tension:
Silence can defuse tension and diffuse conflicts. When faced with a heated exchange or an impasse, a well-timed pause can break the cycle of escalating emotions and create space for rational dialogue. The Sales Samurai recognises that silence can be a powerful tool to de-escalate conflicts, allowing negotiators to regain composure, gather their thoughts, and approach the situation with a calm and focused demeanour. By using silence as a strategic intervention, negotiators can guide the negotiation towards a more constructive path.

Inviting the Other Party's Perspective:
Silence can be used to invite the other party to share their perspective more fully. By consciously remaining silent after a question or statement, negotiators allow the other party to reflect and respond in their own time. This encourages the expression of thoughts, concerns, and interests that might otherwise remain unvoiced. The Sales Samurai emphasises the

importance of creating space for the other party to contribute, fostering a more collaborative and inclusive negotiation environment.

Gaining Information:
Silence can be an effective tool for gathering information and eliciting important details. By pausing and maintaining silence, negotiators encourage the other party to fill the void with additional information or concessions. This can provide valuable insights into the other party's position, interests, and priorities, empowering negotiators to make more informed decisions. The Sales Samurai advises negotiators to use silence strategically to gather information and gain a deeper understanding of the negotiation landscape.

Enhancing Negotiation Strategies:
Silence can enhance negotiation strategies by allowing negotiators to maintain control, create impact, and respond strategically. The Sales Samurai encourages negotiators to utilize silence strategically during critical moments in the negotiation process. Whether it is during the presentation of a proposal, a counteroffer, or a challenging question, a well-pl aced pause can create a sense of anticipation and command attention. By strategically incorporating moments of silence, negotiators can make a powerful impact and influence the direction of the negotiation. Silence can also serve as a tool for negotiation tactics such as mirroring, where negotiators reflect the other party's statements or questions back to them in a thoughtful pause, encouraging further elaboration or clarification.

Cultivating Mindfulness:
Silence provides an opportunity to cultivate mindfulness in negotiation. The Sales Samurai recognises the importance of being fully present in the negotiation process, attuned to the present moment and the dynamics at play. By embracing moments of silence, negotiators can anchor themselves in the here and now, focusing their attention on the nuances of the conversation, the non-verbal cues, and the unspoken messages. Mindfulness allows negotiators to respond authentically, make better judgments, and build stronger connections with the other party.

Exercising Emotional Control:

Silence can be a powerful ally in maintaining emotional control during negotiations. The Sales Samurai acknowledges that negotiations can be emotionally charged, and the ability to regulate emotions is crucial for successful outcomes. By utilizing moments of silence, negotiators can regain composure, prevent impulsive reactions, and respond in a measured and thoughtful manner. Silence acts as a buffer, providing negotiators with the space to manage their emotions and make rational decisions.

Leveraging Non-Verbal Communication:
Silence amplifies the impact of non-verbal communication. The Sales Samurai recognises that communication is not limited to words alone; body language, facial expressions, and gestures also convey important messages. By embracing silence, negotiators can pay closer attention to non-verbal cues, allowing for a deeper understanding of the other party's intentions, emotions, and level of engagement. Non-verbal cues can provide valuable insights that inform negotiation strategies and help negotiators adapt their approach for better results.

Instilling Confidence and Authority:
Strategic use of silence can instil a sense of confidence and authority in negotiators. The Sales Samurai understands that silence can be a display of strength and control, conveying a message of thoughtfulness and deliberation. By employing well-timed pauses, negotiators exude a sense of self-assurance, which can influence the perception of their credibility and expertise. Silence can create a space for negotiators to project confidence and establish themselves as authoritative figures in the negotiation process.

Silence is a powerful tool that the Sales Samurai embraces to enhance communication, gain insights, and achieve favourable outcomes in negotiations. By harnessing the power of pause, negotiators can engage in active listening, strategically reflect, defuse tension, invite the other party's perspective, gain information, enhance negotiation strategies, cultivate mindfulness, exercise emotional control, leverage non-verbal communication, and instil confidence and authority. Mastery of the way of silence empowers negotiators to navigate negotiations with wisdom, clarity, and effectiveness. In the next chapter, we will explore the art of ethical persuasion, equipping negotiators with the skills to influence and persuade others in a principled and respectful manner.

# CHAPTER 11 – THE ART OF QUESTIONING: UNCOVERING HIDDEN OPPORTUNITIES

Sales Samurai understand that the art of questioning is a powerful tool for uncovering hidden opportunities and gaining valuable insights. Chapter 11 explores the philosophy and strategies behind effective questioning techniques. The Sales Samurai recognises that well-crafted questions can reveal unspoken needs, motivations, and priorities, paving the way for mutually beneficial outcomes. By mastering the art of questioning, negotiators can navigate negotiations with precision, uncover hidden value, and forge stronger connections with the other party.

The Power of Questions:

Questions serve as gateways to deeper understanding and meaningful conversations. They have the ability to challenge assumptions, stimulate critical thinking, and uncover valuable information that might otherwise remain hidden. The Sales Samurai understands that asking the right questions at the right time can lead to breakthroughs, creative solutions, and enhanced negotiation outcomes.

Crafting Powerful Questions:

Open-Ended Questions:
Open-ended questions encourage the other party to provide detailed and thoughtful responses. They invite the sharing of perspectives, experiences, and insights, opening up avenues for exploration and understanding. The Sales Samurai encourages negotiators to utilize open-ended questions to gather comprehensive information and gain a deeper understanding of the other party's interests and goals.

Probing Questions:
Probing questions delve deeper into specific areas of interest or concern. They are designed to uncover hidden motivations, explore underlying needs, and challenge assumptions. Probing questions can be used to clarify vague statements, challenge inconsistencies, and prompt the other party to articulate their thoughts more fully. The Sales Samurai emphasises the importance of using probing questions to reveal valuable insights and move the negotiation forward.

Reflective Questions:
Reflective questions encourage introspection and self-reflection. They prompt the other party to consider their own perspectives, assumptions, and biases. Reflective questions can be powerful tools for shifting perspectives, challenging preconceived notions, and fostering mutual understanding. The Sales Samurai encourages negotiators to use reflective questions to promote self-awareness and uncover new possibilities.

Hypothetical Questions:
Hypothetical questions allow negotiators to explore potential scenarios and gauge the other party's responses. They provide a safe space for discussing sensitive or complex issues by framing them in hypothetical terms. Hypothetical questions can help negotiators assess risks, test proposed solutions, and stimulate creative thinking. The Sales Samurai advises negotiators to employ hypothetical questions to encourage open dialogue and foster innovative problem-solving.

Empathetic Questions:

Empathetic questions demonstrate genuine interest and empathy towards the other party's experiences and emotions. They create a supportive and collaborative atmosphere, allowing the other party to feel heard and understood. Empathetic questions can uncover underlying concerns, build trust, and foster a sense of partnership. The Sales Samurai highlights the importance of using empathetic questions to establish rapport and strengthen the negotiation relationship.

Strategic Questions:
Strategic questions are designed to influence the direction of the negotiation and shape the other party's thinking. They are crafted with the intention of guiding the conversation towards desired outcomes. Strategic questions can challenge assumptions, highlight potential advantages, and encourage the other party to consider different perspectives. The Sales Samurai encourages negotiators to use strategic questions to influence the negotiation dynamics and steer towards mutually beneficial solutions.

Uncovering Hidden Opportunities:

Identifying Unmet Needs:
Effective questioning uncovers unmet needs and unspoken desires. By asking probing questions, negotiators can explore the other party's motivations and identify areas where their needs are not being fully met. This opens the door for creative problem-solving and the development of mutually beneficial solutions.

Revealing Interests and Priorities:
Strategic questioning reveals the other party's interests and priorities. By asking open-ended and reflective questions, negotiators can uncover the underlying motivations and priorities that drive the other party's decision-making. This insight allows negotiators to align their proposals and offers with the other party's key interests, increasing the likelihood of reaching a mutually satisfactory agreement.

Exploring Alternative Perspectives:
Well-crafted questions encourage the exploration of alternative perspectives and challenge conventional thinking. By posing hypothetical

and reflective questions, negotiators can invite the other party to consider different possibilities and evaluate the potential benefits of alternative approaches. This expands the scope of the negotiation and opens up opportunities for innovative solutions that may have otherwise been overlooked.

Unearthing Hidden Value:
Through strategic questioning, negotiators can uncover hidden value that can be leveraged for mutual gain. By delving deeper into the other party's needs, preferences, and constraints, negotiators can identify areas where additional value can be created or exchanged. This may involve exploring complementary interests, packaging multiple issues together, or discovering trade-offs that satisfy both parties' objectives. The Sales Samurai understands that unearthing hidden value requires a keen ability to ask insightful questions that elicit meaningful responses.

Resolving Misunderstandings:
Questions play a crucial role in resolving misunderstandings and clarifying miscommunications. When conflicts arise or when there is ambiguity in the negotiation process, well-crafted questions can help identify the root cause of the issue and facilitate a shared understanding. By seeking clarification and asking for additional information, negotiators can address misconceptions and ensure that both parties are on the same page. This promotes a more constructive and effective negotiation environment.

Building Trust and Rapport:
The art of questioning is not solely about gathering information; it also serves as a means to build trust and rapport with the other party. By asking empathetic and open-ended questions, negotiators demonstrate a genuine interest in the other party's perspective and experiences. This fosters a sense of collaboration and respect, establishing a foundation of trust that enhances the negotiation process. The Sales Samurai recognises that building a positive relationship through effective questioning can lead to more fruitful and productive negotiations.

Mastering the Art of Questioning:

Active Listening:
Effective questioning is closely tied to active listening. The Sales Samurai emphasises the importance of fully engaging in the conversation, paying attention to verbal and non-verbal cues, and responding thoughtfully. Active listening enables negotiators to ask relevant and follow-up questions that demonstrate their understanding and facilitate deeper exploration.

Preparation:
Preparation is key to mastering the art of questioning. Before entering a negotiation, negotiators should identify the key information they seek, anticipate potential areas of interest, and craft a set of well-thought-out questions. This preparation allows negotiators to be proactive and strategic in their approach, ensuring that they uncover the information they need to drive the negotiation towards a successful outcome.

Flexibility and Adaptability:
The Sales Samurai understands that effective questioning requires adaptability. Negotiators should be prepared to adjust their questioning strategy based on the dynamics of the negotiation and the responses of the other party. Being flexible allows negotiators to navigate unexpected turns, seize opportunities as they arise, and maintain a collaborative atmosphere throughout the negotiation process.

Emotional Intelligence:
Emotional intelligence plays a vital role in the art of questioning. By being attuned to the emotions and reactions of the other party, negotiators can adjust their questioning approach accordingly. This involves being sensitive to the other party's comfort level, knowing when to ask more challenging questions, and employing empathy to create a safe and constructive environment for dialogue.

The art of questioning is a powerful tool in the Sales Samurai's arsenal. By asking well-crafted questions, negotiators can uncover hidden opportunities, gain valuable insights, and forge stronger connections with the other party. The ability to listen actively, prepare strategically, adapt flexibly, and demonstrate emotional intelligence empowers negotiators to navigate negotiations with precision and effectiveness. The Sales Samurai understands that the art of questioning goes beyond simply gathering information; it is a skill that enables negotiators to uncover hidden value, resolve misunderstandings, and build trust.

By mastering the art of questioning, negotiators can uncover unmet needs and motivations, revealing opportunities for creative problem-solving and win-win outcomes. Strategic questioning also encourages the exploration of alternative perspectives, expanding the range of possible solutions and increasing the likelihood of reaching mutually beneficial agreements.

In addition, effective questioning helps negotiators unearth hidden value by delving deeper into the other party's needs, preferences, and constraints. This allows negotiators to identify areas where additional value can be created or exchanged, leading to more favourable negotiation outcomes for both parties.

Moreover, the art of questioning is a valuable tool in resolving misunderstandings and clarifying miscommunications. By asking for clarification and seeking additional information, negotiators can address misconceptions and ensure that both parties have a shared understanding. This promotes a more constructive and productive negotiation environment, fostering open communication and reducing the risk of conflicts.

Furthermore, skilful questioning contributes to building trust and rapport with the other party. By asking empathetic and open-ended questions, negotiators demonstrate their genuine interest in the other party's perspective and experiences. This creates a sense of collaboration and respect, establishing a foundation of trust that enhances the negotiation process.

To master the art of questioning, negotiators should practice active listening, attentively focusing on verbal and non-verbal cues to respond thoughtfully and ask relevant follow-up questions. Preparation is also crucial, as it allows negotiators to identify the key information they seek and craft well-thought-out questions in advance. Being flexible and adaptable is essential, as negotiators must adjust their questioning approach based on the dynamics of the negotiation and the responses of the other party. Finally, emotional intelligence plays a vital role, enabling negotiators to be sensitive to the other party's emotions, adjust their questioning style accordingly, and create a safe and constructive negotiation environment.

We've now explored the art of questioning as a powerful tool for uncovering hidden opportunities and gaining valuable insights in negotiations. The Sales Samurai emphasises the importance of asking well-crafted questions that encourage open dialogue, challenge assumptions, and stimulate critical thinking. By mastering the art of questioning, negotiators can navigate negotiations with precision, uncover hidden value, and build stronger connections with the other party. The ability to listen actively, prepare strategically, adapt flexibly, and demonstrate emotional intelligence empowers negotiators to achieve successful outcomes and cultivate mutually beneficial agreements.

# CHAPTER 12 – NEGOTIATION TACTICS: A SAMURAI'S ARSENAL

The Sales Samurai understands the importance of employing effective tactics to navigate the complexities of the negotiation process. This chapter explores a variety of negotiation tactics that can be utilised to achieve favourable outcomes. These tactics, akin to a Samurai's arsenal, provide negotiators with the tools and strategies to influence, persuade, and create mutually beneficial agreements. By mastering these tactics, negotiators can navigate negotiations with confidence, adaptability, and strategic thinking.

Anchoring:
Anchoring is a tactic that involves setting a reference point or starting point for negotiations. The Sales Samurai recognises that the initial offer or proposal sets the tone for the rest of the negotiation. By strategically anchoring with a favourable starting point, negotiators can influence the perception of value and guide the negotiation towards more favourable outcomes. Anchoring can be used to create a psychological advantage and shape the other party's expectations.

Framing:

Framing is a tactic that involves presenting information or issues in a particular context to shape the other party's perception and decision-making. The Sales Samurai understands that how negotiators frame their arguments or proposals can influence the interpretation and evaluation of the information. By framing the negotiation in a positive light, emphasising benefits, and highlighting shared interests, negotiators can steer the conversation towards mutually beneficial solutions.

Building Rapport:
Building rapport is a tactic that focuses on establishing a positive and trusting relationship with the other party. The Sales Samurai recognises that trust and rapport contribute to a more collaborative and constructive negotiation environment. By finding common ground, demonstrating empathy, and engaging in active listening, negotiators can foster a sense of partnership and create a foundation for successful negotiations.

Active Listening:
Active listening is a tactic that involves fully engaging in the conversation and attentively understanding the other party's perspective and needs. The Sales Samurai understands that by actively listening, negotiators can gather valuable information, uncover underlying interests, and demonstrate respect for the other party's views. Active listening allows negotiators to respond thoughtfully and tailor their negotiation strategies to the specific needs and concerns of the other party.

Mirroring:
Mirroring is a tactic that involves reflecting the other party's behaviour, language, or gestures to create a sense of rapport and connection. The Sales Samurai recognises that mirroring can help establish a level of comfort and trust with the other party. By adopting a similar communication style or body language, negotiators can create a subconscious bond and increase the likelihood of reaching mutually satisfactory agreements.

Creating Value:
Creating value is a tactic that focuses on expanding the pie and finding opportunities for mutual gain. The Sales Samurai understands that negotiations should not be limited to a zero-sum game but rather aim to

create additional value for both parties. By identifying shared interests, exploring creative solutions, and engaging in collaborative problem-solving, negotiators can achieve outcomes that maximize overall benefits.

Managing Concessions:
Managing concessions is a tactic that involves strategically giving and receiving concessions throughout the negotiation process. The Sales Samurai recognises that concessions should be used strategically to maintain leverage and trade-offs that are favourable to both parties. By managing concessions effectively, negotiators can build momentum, show flexibility, and reach mutually satisfactory agreements without compromising their bottom line.

Overcoming Obstacles:
Overcoming obstacles is a tactic that focuses on addressing and resolving challenges that arise during negotiations. The Sales Samurai understands that obstacles can hinder progress and derail negotiations. By employing problem-solving techniques, actively seeking common ground, and maintaining a constructive mindset, negotiators can navigate through obstacles and find solutions that satisfy both parties' interests.

Managing Time:
Managing time is a tactic that involves skilfully utilizing time as a strategic resource in negotiations. The Sales Samurai recognises that time can exert pressure and influence the negotiation process. Negotiators must be mindful of time constraints and use them to their advantage. By setting deadlines, creating a sense of urgency, and effectively managing the negotiation timeline, negotiators can influence decision-making and drive the negotiation towards timely and favourable outcomes.

Leveraging Information:
Leveraging Information is a tactic that involves utilizing relevant data, facts, and market intelligence to strengthen one's position and influence the negotiation. The Sales Samurai understands that knowledge is power and being well-informed gives negotiators a competitive edge. By conducting thorough research, gathering relevant information, and strategically

presenting data, negotiators can bolster their arguments, increase credibility, and persuade the other party to accept favourable terms.

Using Persuasive Language:
Using persuasive language is a tactic that focuses on employing effective communication techniques to influence the other party's perception and decision-making. The Sales Samurai recognises the power of words and how they can shape the negotiation dynamics. By using persuasive language, such as framing arguments positively, using compelling storytelling, and employing logical reasoning, negotiators can enhance their persuasive abilities and increase the likelihood of reaching agreement on favourable terms.

Managing Emotions:
Managing emotions is a tactic that involves maintaining emotional control and effectively dealing with strong emotions during negotiations. The Sales Samurai understands that emotions can impact decision-making and the negotiation process. By practicing emotional intelligence, staying composed, and adopting a calm and rational demeanour, negotiators can navigate through emotional challenges, de-escalate tense situations, and maintain a productive negotiation environment.

Building Coalitions:
Building coalitions is a tactic that involves forming alliances or partnerships with other stakeholders to strengthen one's position and influence the negotiation. The Sales Samurai recognises that negotiations often involve multiple parties with varying interests. By identifying potential allies, building relationships, and aligning interests, negotiators can create a collective force that amplifies their influence and increases the likelihood of achieving their objectives.

Assessing Power Dynamics:
Assessing power dynamics is a tactic that involves understanding the relative power and leverage of each party in the negotiation. The Sales Samurai recognises that power imbalances can significantly impact the negotiation outcomes. By carefully analysing the sources of power, identifying strengths and weaknesses, and developing strategies to level the

playing field, negotiators can navigate power dynamics effectively and negotiate from a position of strength.

These tactics equip negotiators with the tools and strategies to influence, persuade, and create mutually beneficial agreements. By mastering these tactics, negotiators can navigate negotiations with confidence, adaptability, and strategic thinking. Anchoring, framing, building rapport, active listening, mirroring, creating value, managing concessions, overcoming obstacles, managing time, leveraging information, using persuasive language, managing emotions, building coalitions, and assessing power dynamics are tactics that enable negotiators to maximize their negotiation outcomes. The Sales Samurai understands that employing these tactics requires a balance of skill, preparation, and ethical conduct. By incorporating these tactics into their negotiation approach, negotiators can become formidable and effective in achieving successful negotiation outcomes.

# CHAPTER 13 – NEGOTIATING WITH HONOUR: ETHICAL PRINCIPLES FOR SALES SAMURAI

Ethics and integrity are paramount in the practice of negotiation. In this Chapter, we delve into the ethical principles that guide the Sales Samurai in their negotiations. The Sales Samurai understands that true success is not measured solely by the outcome of a negotiation but also by the integrity and fairness with which it is conducted. By upholding ethical principles, negotiators can build trust, maintain long-term relationships, and create win-win solutions that benefit all parties involved.

Honesty and Transparency:
Honesty and transparency form the foundation of ethical negotiation. The Sales Samurai values open and truthful communication, providing accurate information and avoiding misleading statements or omissions. By fostering an atmosphere of trust through honest and transparent exchanges, negotiators can establish a strong rapport and facilitate constructive dialogue that leads to mutually beneficial agreements.

Respect and Dignity:

Respect and dignity are fundamental ethical principles in negotiation. The Sales Samurai recognises the inherent worth and value of all parties involved. Negotiators treat others with respect, listen attentively, and consider diverse perspectives. By demonstrating empathy, valuing the contributions of all stakeholders, and maintaining a respectful approach, negotiators can foster a positive negotiation climate that encourages cooperation and collaboration.

Fairness and Equity:
Fairness and equity are essential ethical principles that guide the Sales Samurai. Negotiators strive to ensure a fair distribution of benefits and costs among all parties involved. The Sales Samurai avoids unfair advantage-seeking tactics and seeks to create agreements that promote equitable outcomes. By upholding fairness and equity, negotiators cultivate a sense of fairness and goodwill, laying the groundwork for successful long-term relationships.

Integrity and Professionalism:
Integrity and professionalism are integral to the Sales Samurai's negotiation practice. The Sales Samurai conducts negotiations with the utmost integrity, adhering to ethical standards and moral principles. Negotiators act in a professional manner, honouring commitments, and maintaining confidentiality when required. By embodying integrity and professionalism, negotiators establish a reputation for trustworthiness and reliability, which is crucial in building lasting business relationships.

Collaboration and Win-Win Solutions:
Collaboration and win-win solutions are at the heart of ethical negotiation. The Sales Samurai recognises that negotiation is not a zero-sum game but an opportunity for mutual benefit. Negotiators actively seek to understand the interests and needs of all parties involved and work towards solutions that satisfy everyone's objectives. By prioritising collaboration and win win outcomes, negotiators foster a cooperative spirit, promote long-term success, and nurture productive business partnerships.

Ethical Use of Power:

The Sales Samurai understands the ethical responsibility that comes with wielding power in negotiation. Negotiators avoid exploiting power imbalances or engaging in manipulative tactics. Instead, they use their power to create value, seek common ground, and ensure that all parties have an equal opportunity to contribute and benefit. By employing power ethically, negotiators cultivate an environment of trust and fairness, paving the way for sustainable agreements.

Responsibility and Accountability:
Responsibility and accountability are crucial ethical principles for the Sales Samurai. Negotiators take responsibility for their actions, decisions, and their impact on all stakeholders. They are accountable for fulfilling their commitments and obligations. By embracing responsibility and accountability, negotiators demonstrate their commitment to ethical conduct and build credibility and trust among their counterparts.

Ethical Decision-Making:
Ethical decision-making is a fundamental skill for the Sales Samurai. Negotiators analyse the ethical implications of their choices and consider the potential consequences for all parties involved. They prioritise long-term relationships and shared values over short-term gains. By incorporating ethical considerations into their decision-making process, negotiators uphold their integrity and make choices that align with their values.

Chapter 13 emphasises the importance of ethical principles in the negotiation practice of the Sales Samurai. By adhering to honesty and transparency, respect and dignity, fairness and equity, integrity and professionalism, collaboration and win-win solutions, ethical use of power, responsibility and accountability, and ethical decision-making, negotiators can create a negotiation environment that is rooted in integrity and fosters trust and cooperation.

The Sales Samurai understands that ethical negotiation is not only about achieving favourable outcomes but also about maintaining strong relationships and upholding a reputation for fairness and trustworthiness.

By consistently applying these ethical principles, negotiators can navigate negotiations with integrity, even in challenging situations. They prioritise the long-term implications of their actions and strive to create solutions that benefit all parties involved.

Ethical negotiation is not always the easiest path. It may require compromise, creative problem-solving, and a willingness to consider alternative perspectives. However, the Sales Samurai knows that ethical conduct is essential for building sustainable business relationships and achieving long-term success. By consistently embodying these ethical principles, negotiators differentiate themselves as trusted and respected professionals in the field of negotiation.

Furthermore, ethical negotiation is not confined to individual transactions or deals. The Sales Samurai recognises the broader societal impact of their negotiation practices. They understand that their actions can shape business cultures, influence industry norms, and contribute to the overall well-being of stakeholders and communities. By conducting negotiations with honour, negotiators can be catalysts for positive change and promote a more ethical and equitable business environment.

To integrate ethical principles into their negotiation approach, the Sales Samurai continually assess their actions and decisions. They reflect on their conduct, seek feedback from others, and learn from their experiences. They also stay informed about evolving ethical standards and best practices in negotiation, remaining adaptable and open to improvement.

These are the ethical principles that guide the Sales Samurai in their negotiation practice. By upholding honesty and transparency, respect and dignity, fairness and equity, integrity and professionalism, collaboration and win-win solutions, ethical use of power, responsibility and accountability, and ethical decision-making, negotiators can build trust, maintain long-term relationships, and achieve outcomes that align with their values. The Sales Samurai recognises that ethical conduct in negotiation is not just a means to an end but an intrinsic part of their identity and a reflection of their commitment to integrity and excellence. By embodying these ethical principles, negotiators become exemplars of ethical negotiation and contribute to a more ethical and sustainable business landscape.

# The 7 virtues of the Samurai

*"Gi"*

*Justice & Rectitude.*
Rightness or correctness in judgment

*"Rei"*

*Courtesy & Respect.*
Polite, considerate behavior to others

*"Yu"*

*Valor & Courage.*
Determination in the face of danger

*"Makoto"*

*Honesty & Veracity.*
Habitual observance of truth

*"Jin"*

*Benevolence & Compassion.*
Giving to the less fortunate

*"Meiyo"*

*Honor & Resolve.*
Integrity of one's actions

*"Chungi"*

*Loyalty & Dedication.*
Selfless devotion

# CHAPTER 14 – OVERCOMING OBSTACLES: RESILIENCE AND ADAPTABILITY IN NEGOTIATIONS

Negotiations can often present various challenges and obstacles that require resilience and adaptability to overcome. In Chapter 14, we explore the importance of resilience and adaptability in the negotiation process. The Sales Samurai understands that the ability to navigate through setbacks, overcome obstacles, and adapt to changing circumstances is essential for achieving successful outcomes. By cultivating resilience and embracing adaptability, negotiators can maintain a competitive edge and maximize their chances of reaching favourable agreements.

Understanding the Nature of Obstacles:
The Sales Samurai recognises that obstacles are inevitable in negotiations. These obstacles can take the form of differing interests, conflicting priorities, resistance, or external factors beyond one's control. Understanding the nature of obstacles is crucial for developing effective strategies to address them. The Sales Samurai remains proactive in identifying potential

challenges, analysing their root causes, and devising creative solutions to overcome them.

Embracing a Growth Mindset:
A growth mindset is a fundamental quality for the Sales Samurai when faced with obstacles. Instead of viewing obstacles as insurmountable barriers, negotiators with a growth mindset see them as opportunities for learning and growth. They approach challenges with curiosity and a willingness to adapt their strategies. By embracing a growth mindset, negotiators can transform setbacks into stepping stones and leverage their experiences to enhance future negotiations.

Flexibility and Adaptability:
Flexibility and adaptability are key attributes of the Sales Samurai. Negotiators must be prepared to adjust their approaches and strategies in response to changing circumstances. They recognise that rigidity can hinder progress and limit opportunities for creative problem-solving. By remaining flexible and adaptable, negotiators can find alternative paths, explore new options, and maintain momentum even in the face of unexpected challenges.

Resilience in the Face of Setbacks:
Resilience is an essential trait for the Sales Samurai. Negotiators must be able to bounce back from setbacks, setbacks, and maintain a positive mindset. They view setbacks as temporary and see them as opportunities to reassess their strategies and find new ways forward. By developing resilience, negotiators can maintain motivation, stay focused on their objectives, and persevere through difficulties with determination and optimism.

Effective Communication and Relationship Building:
Effective communication and relationship building are critical for overcoming obstacles in negotiations. The Sales Samurai recognises that open and honest communication is key to resolving conflicts and finding common ground. Negotiators actively listen, seek to understand the perspectives of others, and foster a collaborative environment. By building

strong relationships based on trust and respect, negotiators can navigate through obstacles more effectively and find mutually agreeable solutions.

Problem-Solving and Creativity:
Problem-solving and creativity are invaluable skills for the Sales Samurai when faced with obstacles. Negotiators approach challenges with a solution-oriented mindset and seek innovative ways to address them. They think outside the box, explore different perspectives, and consider alternative options. By leveraging their creativity and problem-solving abilities, negotiators can overcome obstacles and find win-win solutions that meet the interests of all parties involved.

Learning from Experience:
The Sales Samurai understands the importance of learning from past experiences. Negotiators reflect on their successes and failures, extracting valuable lessons to improve their negotiation skills. They continually seek feedback, evaluate their performance, and make adjustments accordingly. By embracing a learning mindset, negotiators can refine their approaches, strengthen their resilience, and enhance their adaptability in future negotiations.

Seeking Support and Collaboration:
The Sales Samurai recognises the value of seeking support and collaboration when faced with significant obstacles. Negotiators understand that they do not have to face challenges alone. They seek input from mentors, colleagues, or subject matter experts who can offer guidance and perspective. By leveraging the collective wisdom and support of others, negotiators can gain new insights, identify alternative approaches, and increase their chances of overcoming obstacles.

Maintaining a Long-Term Perspective:
The Sales Samurai maintains a long-term perspective when confronted with obstacles. Negotiators understand that negotiations are not isolated events but part of ongoing relationships and partnerships. They prioritise the preservation of relationships and seek solutions that consider the long-term implications. By taking a holistic view and considering the broader context,

negotiators can find innovative ways to address obstacles while preserving the foundation for future collaborations.

Embracing Change and Uncertainty:
Change and uncertainty are inherent in negotiations, and the Sales Samurai embraces them with adaptability and resilience. Negotiators recognise that change can present both challenges and opportunities. They remain open to new possibilities, adjust their strategies as needed, and proactively anticipate and address potential uncertainties. By embracing change and uncertainty, negotiators position themselves to navigate through obstacles with agility and confidence.

Maintaining Self-Care and Well-being:
The Sales Samurai understands the importance of self-care and well-being in overcoming obstacles. Negotiations can be mentally and emotionally demanding, and negotiators must prioritise their physical and mental health. They engage in self-care practices such as exercise, mindfulness, and stress management techniques. By maintaining their well-being, negotiators enhance their resilience, decision-making abilities, and overall effectiveness in managing obstacles.

Hopefully this highlights the significance of resilience and adaptability in navigating through obstacles in negotiations. The Sales Samurai recognises that obstacles are an inevitable part of the negotiation process, but they do not have to be insurmountable barriers. By understanding the nature of obstacles, embracing a growth mindset, remaining flexible and adaptable, maintaining resilience in the face of setbacks, fostering effective communication and relationship building, leveraging problem-solving and creativity, learning from experience, seeking support and collaboration, maintaining a long-term perspective, embracing change and uncertainty, and prioritising self-care, negotiators can overcome obstacles and achieve successful outcomes.

The Sales Samurai views obstacles as opportunities for growth, innovation, and building stronger relationships. They approach challenges with resilience and adaptability, finding creative solutions that meet the interests of all parties involved. By cultivating these qualities, negotiators position themselves as skilled and capable professionals who can navigate through obstacles with confidence, integrity, and success.

# CHAPTER 15 – NEGOTIATING ACROSS CULTURES: INSIGHTS FOR GLOBAL SAMURAI

In today's interconnected and globalized world, the ability to negotiate effectively across cultures is a critical skill for the Global Samurai. Chapter 15 explores the nuances and challenges of negotiating across different cultural contexts. The Global Samurai recognises that cultural differences can significantly impact negotiation dynamics, communication styles, and the interpretation of verbal and non-verbal cues. By gaining insights into cultural nuances and adapting their approach accordingly, negotiators can bridge cultural gaps, build trust, and achieve successful outcomes in cross-cultural negotiations.

Cultural Awareness and Sensitivity:
The Global Samurai understands the importance of cultural awareness and sensitivity. Negotiators recognise that different cultures have distinct values,

beliefs, and communication styles. They invest time in learning about the cultural norms, customs, and etiquette of their counterparts. By demonstrating respect for cultural differences, negotiators lay the foundation for effective cross-cultural negotiations.

Building Trust and Rapport:
Building trust and rapport is crucial when negotiating across cultures. The Global Samurai recognises that trust takes time to establish, particularly in cross-cultural contexts. Negotiators prioritise relationship-building, investing in face-to-face interactions whenever possible. They demonstrate genuine interest in the other party's culture, actively listen, and seek to understand their perspectives. By building trust and rapport, negotiators create a conducive environment for open and productive negotiations.

Communication Styles and Language:
Effective communication is a key aspect of cross-cultural negotiation. The Global Samurai understands that communication styles can vary significantly across cultures. Negotiators adapt their communication approach to accommodate the preferences of their counterparts. They strive for clarity, avoiding ambiguous language or idiomatic expressions that may be challenging to understand. By being mindful of language and communication styles, negotiators enhance mutual understanding and minimize misunderstandings.

Non-Verbal Communication:
Non-verbal communication plays a vital role in cross-cultural negotiations. The Global Samurai recognises that gestures, body language, and facial expressions can convey different meanings in different cultures. Negotiators pay attention to non-verbal cues and adapt their own behaviour accordingly. They avoid assumptions and seek clarification when interpreting non-verbal signals. By being attuned to non-verbal communication, negotiators can enhance their understanding and foster effective cross-cultural communication.

Cultural Norms and Decision-Making:
Cultural norms and decision-making processes vary across cultures, and the Global Samurai is sensitive to these differences. Negotiators understand

that some cultures prioritise consensus-building and group harmony, while others emphasise individual decision-making and assertiveness. They adapt their negotiation strategies to align with cultural preferences, respecting the decision-making norms of their counterparts. By acknowledging and accommodating cultural norms, negotiators create an atmosphere conducive to mutual agreement.

Patience and Flexibility:
Patience and flexibility are essential qualities for the Global Samurai in cross-cultural negotiations. Negotiators understand that negotiations across cultures may require more time and flexibility than those within a single cultural context. They exhibit patience in navigating cultural differences, allowing space for clarifications, and accommodating differing viewpoints. By being patient and flexible, negotiators demonstrate a willingness to adapt and find mutually beneficial solutions.

Negotiating with Cultural Context in Mind:
The Global Samurai negotiates with the cultural context in mind. Negotiators conduct thorough research on the cultural background of the parties involved and the specific cultural context of the negotiation. They avoid assumptions or stereotypes and approach negotiations with cultural sensitivity. By understanding the cultural context, negotiators can tailor their strategies, anticipate potential challenges, and effectively navigate cultural nuances.

Embracing Cultural Learning Opportunities:
The Global Samurai embraces cultural learning opportunities as a means to improve their cross-cultural negotiation skills. Negotiators actively seek experiences that expose them to diverse cultures and engage in intercultural training programs. They continually seek feedback and learn from their experiences in cross-cultural negotiations. By embracing cultural learning opportunities, negotiators expand their cultural knowledge, enhance their understanding of different perspectives, and refine their cross-cultural negotiation skills.

Adapting to Local Business Practices:

Adapting to local business practices is crucial when negotiating across cultures. The Global Samurai recognises that business customs and practices can vary significantly from one culture to another. Negotiators strive to understand the local business environment, including protocols for greetings, gift-giving, and negotiation styles. By respecting and adapting to local practices, negotiators demonstrate cultural sensitivity and foster positive relationships with their counterparts.

Managing Conflict and Resolving Differences:
Conflict is an inevitable part of negotiations, and the Global Samurai understands how to manage it effectively in cross-cultural settings. Negotiators approach conflict with cultural sensitivity, seeking win-win solutions that consider the interests and values of all parties involved. They employ active listening, empathy, and collaborative problem-solving techniques to address and resolve differences. By managing conflict in a culturally sensitive manner, negotiators maintain the integrity of the negotiation process and preserve relationships.

Leveraging Cultural Diversity as a Strength:
The Global Samurai views cultural diversity as a strength rather than a challenge in cross-cultural negotiations. Negotiators recognise that diverse perspectives and approaches can lead to innovative solutions and opportunities for mutual learning. They leverage cultural diversity to foster creativity, adaptability, and out-of-the-box thinking. By embracing cultural diversity, negotiators can harness the full potential of cross-cultural negotiations and achieve outcomes that are inclusive and beneficial for all parties involved.

Reflecting on Ethical Implications:
Ethics play a crucial role in cross-cultural negotiations, and the Global Samurai reflects on the ethical implications of their actions. Negotiators strive to maintain integrity, fairness, and respect for cultural values throughout the negotiation process. They navigate cultural differences with ethical sensitivity, ensuring that their actions align with ethical principles and standards. By reflecting on ethical implications, negotiators uphold their reputation as ethical and trustworthy professionals.

By developing cultural awareness, building trust and rapport, adapting communication styles, understanding non-verbal cues, respecting cultural norms and decision-making processes, practicing patience and flexibility, considering cultural context, embracing cultural learning opportunities, adapting to local business practices, managing conflict, leveraging cultural diversity, and reflecting on ethical implications, negotiators can navigate cross-cultural negotiations with confidence and achieve successful outcomes. The Global Samurai understands that cultural differences provide an opportunity for growth, collaboration, and mutual understanding. By embracing cultural diversity and approaching negotiations with cultural sensitivity, negotiators can foster meaningful connections, build enduring relationships, and excel in the complex landscape of global negotiations.

# CHAPTER 16 – MASTERY IN ACTION: CASE STUDIES OF SALES SAMURAI NEGOTIATIONS

In this Chapter, we delve into real-life case studies showcasing the mastery of Sales Samurai in negotiation. By examining these case studies, we gain valuable insights into the strategies, tactics, and mindset employed by successful negotiators. These stories highlight the application of the Sales Samurai principles and provide practical examples of how negotiators navigate challenges, overcome obstacles, and achieve exceptional results. By studying these case studies, readers can learn from the experiences of Sales Samurai and apply their lessons to their own negotiation practices.

Case Study 1: "The Global Partnership":
In this case study, a Sales Samurai negotiator was tasked with securing a strategic partnership with a multinational corporation. The challenge was to align the interests of both parties while navigating cultural differences and competing priorities. The Sales Samurai leveraged their cultural intelligence, built strong relationships with key stakeholders, and focused on creating a win-win scenario. Through effective communication, creative problem-

solving, and persistence, the negotiator successfully forged a global partnership that exceeded expectations.

Case Study 2: "The Complex Acquisition":
In this case study, a Sales Samurai negotiator was assigned to lead a complex acquisition deal involving multiple parties, intricate financial arrangements, and legal considerations. The negotiator demonstrated exceptional analytical skills, attention to detail, and the ability to manage complexity. They adeptly coordinated various teams, maintained open lines of communication, and addressed concerns from all parties involved. Through meticulous planning, strategic manoeuvring, and skilled negotiation, the Sales Samurai secured a successful acquisition deal that aligned with their client's objectives.

Case Study 3: "The Cross-Cultural Joint Venture":
In this case study, a Sales Samurai negotiator was involved in facilitating a cross-cultural joint venture between two companies from different countries. The negotiator recognised the significance of cultural differences and invested time in building relationships based on trust and respect. They actively listened to the concerns and perspectives of both parties, bridging cultural gaps and finding common ground. Through their cultural sensitivity, adaptability, and skilled negotiation, the Sales Samurai played a pivotal role in establishing a successful joint venture that leveraged the strengths of both organizations.

Case Study 4: "The High-Stakes Contract Renegotiation":
In this case study, a Sales Samurai negotiator was tasked with renegotiating a high-stakes contract with a long-standing client. The challenge was to address changing market dynamics and ensure a mutually beneficial agreement while maintaining a strong relationship. The negotiator demonstrated a deep understanding of the client's needs, industry trends, and market dynamics. Through collaborative problem-solving, effective communication, and a focus on value creation, the Sales Samurai successfully renegotiated the contract, preserving the relationship and securing a favourable outcome for both parties.

Case Study 5: "The Crisis Management Negotiation":

In this case study, a Sales Samurai negotiator found themselves in a crisis management situation that required swift action and skilful negotiation. The negotiator displayed composure, resilience, and adaptability in the face of a challenging situation. They communicated effectively with stakeholders, managed conflicting interests, and made difficult decisions to resolve the crisis. Through their strategic thinking, agility, and ability to find common ground, the Sales Samurai mitigated the crisis and restored trust and stability.

Case Study 6: "The International Trade Agreement":
In this case study, a Sales Samurai negotiator was involved in negotiating an international trade agreement between multiple countries. The negotiator navigated complex political landscapes, differing regulatory frameworks, and competing interests. They demonstrated exceptional diplomatic skills, patience, and perseverance. Through their ability to find mutually beneficial solutions, build consensus, and address concerns of all parties, the Sales Samurai played a pivotal role in facilitating the international trade agreement. Their understanding of cultural nuances, ability to bridge gaps, and commitment to fair and equitable outcomes led to a successful agreement that fostered economic growth and cooperation among the participating countries.

Case Study 7: "The Vendor Partnership":
In this case study, a Sales Samurai negotiator was tasked with establishing a long-term vendor partnership for a client. The negotiator conducted extensive research, identified potential vendors, and conducted thorough due diligence. They approached the negotiation with a collaborative mindset, seeking to build a mutually beneficial partnership. Through effective communication, skilled negotiation, and a focus on shared values and goals, the Sales Samurai secured a vendor partnership that delivered quality products, cost savings, and a competitive advantage for the client.

Case Study 8: "The Salary Negotiation":
In this case study, a Sales Samurai negotiator was faced with a critical salary negotiation. The negotiator employed a strategic approach, conducting thorough market research and leveraging their track record of success. They articulated their value proposition, emphasising their contributions to the

company's growth and success. Through effective communication, persuasive argumentation, and a focus on win-win outcomes, the Sales Samurai negotiated a salary package that reflected their worth and aligned with their career aspirations.

Case Study 9: "The Diplomatic Mediation":
In this case study, a Sales Samurai negotiator was called upon to mediate a dispute between two organizations with conflicting interests. The negotiator assumed a neutral and unbiased position, facilitating open dialogue and fostering a collaborative atmosphere. They employed active listening, empathy, and skilled negotiation techniques to help the parties understand each other's perspectives and find common ground. Through their diplomatic approach and commitment to finding a fair and mutually acceptable resolution, the Sales Samurai successfully mediated the dispute, preserving the relationship between the organizations and paving the way for future collaboration.

Case Study 10: "The Strategic Alliance":
In this case study, a Sales Samurai negotiator played a crucial role in establishing a strategic alliance between two companies in a highly competitive industry. The negotiator conducted extensive market research, identified synergies between the organizations, and crafted a compelling value proposition. They engaged in persuasive negotiations, aligning the interests and objectives of both parties. Through their strategic thinking, innovative problem-solving, and ability to navigate complex negotiations, the Sales Samurai facilitated the formation of a strategic alliance that created significant value and competitive advantage for both organizations.

These examples of real-life case studies showcase the mastery of Sales Samurai in negotiation. Through these case studies, readers gain valuable insights into the strategies, tactics, and mindset employed by successful negotiators. The Sales Samurai demonstrated their ability to navigate diverse challenges, adapt to different contexts, build relationships, and achieve exceptional results. By studying these case studies, readers can extract valuable lessons and apply them to their own negotiation endeavours, paving the way for their own mastery in the art of negotiation.

World figures that demonstrate the Way of the Sales Samurai:

Elon Musk - Known for his visionary leadership and exceptional negotiation skills, Elon Musk has successfully negotiated various deals and partnerships for his companies, such as Tesla and SpaceX. His ability to navigate complex situations, think strategically, and drive win-win outcomes reflects the Sales Samurai ethos.

Oprah Winfrey - As a media mogul and philanthropist, Oprah Winfrey has showcased exceptional negotiation skills throughout her career. Her ability to connect with people, build rapport, and create mutually beneficial partnerships aligns with the Sales Samurai ethos of building relationships and achieving win-win solutions.

Richard Branson - Richard Branson, the founder of Virgin Group, is renowned for his charismatic personality and negotiation prowess. His ability to strike deals, form strategic alliances, and build successful businesses demonstrates the Sales Samurai ethos of strategic thinking, adaptability, and value creation.

Indra Nooyi - Indra Nooyi, the former CEO of PepsiCo, is known for her exceptional leadership and negotiation skills. Her ability to navigate complex business environments, manage stakeholder relationships, and drive sustainable growth aligns with the Sales Samurai ethos of integrity, collaboration, and achieving long-term success.

Warren Buffett - Warren Buffett, one of the world's most successful investors, exemplifies the Sales Samurai ethos through his disciplined approach to negotiation and investing. His emphasis on long-term value creation, patience, and rational decision-making reflects the core principles of the Sales Samurai.

Sheryl Sandberg - Sheryl Sandberg, the Chief Operating Officer of Facebook, is known for her strategic thinking and negotiation skills. Her ability to build strong partnerships, drive innovation, and foster collaboration aligns with the Sales Samurai ethos of forging meaningful connections and achieving mutual success.

Mary Barra - Mary Barra, the CEO of General Motors, demonstrates the Sales Samurai ethos through her leadership in negotiating complex industry deals, adapting to changing market dynamics, and driving organizational transformation. Her focus on customer-centricity, innovation, and sustainability resonates with the core values of the Sales Samurai.

Mark Cuban - Mark Cuban, entrepreneur and owner of the Dallas Mavericks, embodies the Sales Samurai ethos through his negotiation skills and business acumen. His ability to identify opportunities, take calculated risks, and drive successful outcomes aligns with the Sales Samurai principles of adaptability, strategic thinking, and value creation.

Angela Merkel - Angela Merkel, the former Chancellor of Germany, is known for her diplomatic skills and negotiation prowess on the global stage. Her ability to navigate complex political landscapes, build consensus, and drive sustainable outcomes reflects the Sales Samurai ethos of effective communication, collaboration, and problem-solving.

These individuals exemplify the Sales Samurai ethos through their exceptional negotiation skills, strategic thinking, ability to build relationships, and drive for mutual success. By studying their approaches and experiences, one can gain valuable insights into embodying the Sales Samurai mindset and achieving mastery in negotiation.

# CHAPTER 17 – THE ART OF CLOSING: SEALING THE DEAL WITH SALES SAMURAI TECHNIQUES

Now we delve into the crucial phase of negotiation known as "the close." As Sales Samurai, the ability to seal the deal with finesse and confidence is essential for achieving successful outcomes. This chapter focuses on the art of closing, providing Sales Samurai with effective techniques and strategies to secure agreements, reach mutually beneficial outcomes, and solidify relationships. By mastering the art of closing, Sales Samurai can maximize their negotiation results and demonstrate their expertise in the field.

Building Momentum:
Closing a negotiation successfully requires careful attention to building momentum throughout the negotiation process. Sales Samurai understand the importance of creating a sense of progress and alignment leading up to the close. They skilfully navigate the negotiation dynamics, emphasising points of agreement, addressing concerns, and ensuring that all parties feel heard and respected. By building positive momentum, Sales Samurai set the stage for a successful close.

Active Listening and Responding:

Active listening is a powerful tool in the closing phase of a negotiation. Sales Samurai engage in attentive listening, demonstrating genuine interest in the other party's perspectives, needs, and concerns. They use active listening techniques such as paraphrasing, summarizing, and asking clarifying questions to ensure a comprehensive understanding of the other party's position. Sales Samurai respond thoughtfully and empathetically, addressing any remaining issues or objections and showing a willingness to find common ground.

Seeking Win-Win Solutions:
Sales Samurai prioritise win-win outcomes during the closing phase. They understand that reaching a mutually beneficial agreement ensures long-term success and fosters positive relationships. Sales Samurai explore creative solutions and innovative approaches that satisfy the interests of all parties involved. They look for opportunities to expand the pie and identify value-adding elements that can enhance the overall agreement. By focusing on win-win solutions, Sales Samurai demonstrate their commitment to collaborative and sustainable negotiations.

Overcoming Objections:
Objections are a common occurrence during the closing phase of a negotiation. Sales Samurai anticipate objections and are prepared to address them effectively. They approach objections as opportunities to provide additional information, clarify misunderstandings, and alleviate concerns. Sales Samurai respond with confidence and professionalism, presenting well-crafted counterarguments and addressing objections with factual evidence, logical reasoning, and persuasive techniques. By overcoming objections, Sales Samurai move the negotiation closer to a successful close.

Managing Concessions:
Negotiations often involve a process of give-and-take, and Sales Samurai understand the art of managing concessions. They approach concessions strategically, ensuring that each concession they make is purposeful and calculated. Sales Samurai carefully evaluate the value of each concession and consider the potential impact on the overall negotiation outcome. They seek reciprocal concessions from the other party to maintain a balanced

negotiation process. By managing concessions effectively, Sales Samurai navigate the closing phase with tact and skill.

Creating a Sense of Urgency:
Creating a sense of urgency can be a powerful closing technique. Sales Samurai understand the importance of timing and leveraging the right moments to prompt action. They highlight the benefits and advantages of reaching an agreement promptly, emphasising the potential costs or missed opportunities associated with delays. Sales Samurai use persuasive language and storytelling techniques to convey the urgency and inspire the other party to act decisively. By creating a sense of urgency, Sales Samurai motivate the other party to make a final commitment.

Finalizing the Agreement:
The final stage of closing involves finalizing the agreement and ensuring all necessary details are addressed. Sales Samurai approach this phase with meticulous attention to detail, confirming that all terms, conditions, and obligations are clearly defined and documented. They facilitate a smooth transition to the implementation phase by clarifying next steps, timelines, and any necessary follow-up actions. Sales Samurai aim to create a sense of closure and satisfaction for all parties involved, solidifying the agreement and setting the foundation for a successful working relationship.

Leveraging Non-Verbal Communication:
Non-verbal communication plays a significant role in the closing phase of a negotiation. Sales Samurai are mindful of their body language, facial expressions, and overall demeanour. They project confidence, professionalism, and sincerity through their non-verbal cues, reinforcing their commitment to the agreement and establishing trust. Sales Samurai maintain eye contact, use appropriate gestures, and exhibit open and welcoming body language, creating an atmosphere of trust and rapport that supports the closing process.

Handling Final Negotiation Tactics:
During the closing phase, various negotiation tactics may arise, such as last-minute demands, ultimatums, or unexpected concessions from the other party. Sales Samurai are well-prepared to handle these tactics with poise

and strategic thinking. They remain calm and composed, evaluating each situation objectively and responding in a manner that protects their interests while maintaining the integrity of the negotiation process. Sales Samurai avoid impulsive reactions and instead rely on their well-honed negotiation skills to navigate these final challenges and bring the negotiation to a successful close.

Solidifying Relationships:
Closing a negotiation is not only about reaching an agreement but also about solidifying relationships for future collaboration. Sales Samurai recognise the importance of maintaining positive connections beyond the negotiation table. They express gratitude and appreciation for the other party's participation and contributions. Sales Samurai follow up with a clear communication plan, ensuring that both parties are aligned on the next steps and that any necessary post-negotiation actions are executed promptly. By solidifying relationships, Sales Samurai establish a foundation of trust and respect that can lead to future opportunities and mutually beneficial partnerships.

By building momentum, actively listening and responding, seeking win-win solutions, overcoming objections, managing concessions, creating a sense of urgency, finalizing agreements, leveraging non-verbal communication, handling final negotiation tactics, and solidifying relationships, Sales Samurai can master the art of closing and achieve successful outcomes. The chapter emphasises the importance of preparation, strategy, and interpersonal skills in the closing phase of negotiations. By adopting these Sales Samurai techniques, negotiators can enhance their ability to secure agreements, build strong relationships, and establish themselves as skilled and accomplished negotiators.

# CHAPTER 18 – OTHER BOOKS FROM THE TEAM AT SALES SAMURAI

Other resources you might find useful.

"The Way of The Sales Samurai: Unlocking Negotiation Mastery" is a transformative guidebook that takes readers on a journey to master the art of negotiation. Drawing inspiration from the legendary samurai warriors, this book combines ancient wisdom with modern sales strategies to equip readers with the skills and mindset needed to excel in negotiations.

"The Art of Prospecting: Mastering the Sales Samurai's Hunting Techniques" - This book delves into the art of prospecting, teaching Sales Samurai how to identify, engage, and qualify potential leads effectively. It covers strategies for researching prospects, leveraging networking opportunities, and utilizing technology to optimize prospecting efforts. Readers will learn how to build a robust pipeline and increase their chances of closing deals.

"The Sales Samurai's Persuasive Pitch: Crafting Compelling Presentations for Sales Success" - This book focuses on the art of delivering persuasive sales pitches. Sales Samurai will learn how to structure and deliver compelling presentations that engage and influence their audience. It covers techniques for storytelling, addressing customer pain points, showcasing value, and handling objections. Readers will gain insights into creating impactful presentations that resonate with their prospects.

"The Consultative Sales Approach: Unlocking Customer Success Through Sales Samurai Strategies" - This book explores the consultative sales approach, emphasising the importance of understanding customer needs and providing tailored solutions. Sales Samurai will learn how to ask insightful questions, actively listen, and align their offerings with customer objectives. It covers techniques for building trust, conducting effective needs assessments, and positioning products or services as valuable solutions.

"The Mastery of Closing: Sales Samurai Techniques for Securing the Deal" - This book delves into the art of closing sales effectively. It covers a range of closing techniques, from assumptive and alternative closes to trial closes and handling objections. Sales Samurai will learn how to create a sense of urgency, address customer concerns, and navigate the final stages of the sales process. Readers will gain practical strategies for securing commitments and achieving successful sales outcomes.

These additional books in the Sales Samurai series provide valuable insights and strategies for different aspects of the sales process. Readers can enhance their sales skills and techniques, building upon the foundation laid by "The Way of The Sales Samurai: Unlocking Negotiation Mastery."

If you have enjoyed this book and wish to engage with Sales Samurai you can find us online and on all social media platforms.

Sales Samurai offer business training and consulting services in the area of sales strategy, process and development.

www.ingramcontent.com/pod-product-compliance
Lightning Source LLC
Chambersburg PA
CBHW062343290526
45794CB00005B/2091